People of the Ancient World

ANCIENT MESOPOTAMIA

THE SUMERIANS, BABYLONIANS, AND ASSYRIANS

WRITTEN BY
VIRGINIA SCHOMP

Franklin Watts
A Division of Scholastic Inc.
New York Toronto London Auckland Sydney
Mexico City New Delhi Hong Kong
Danbury, Connecticut

To my brother Russ, for that well read library

Note to readers: Definitions for words in **bold** can be found in the Glossary at the back of this book.

Photographs © 2004: Art Resource, NY: 94 bottom (British Museum, London), 74, 77 (Iraq Museum, Baghdad), 66 (Erich Lessing), 53, 68, 69 (Louvre, Paris); Bridgeman Art Library International Ltd., London/New York: 11, 70, 71 (Ashmolean Museum, Oxford, UK), 46, 72, 83 (British Museum, London, UK), 75 (Hermitage, St. Petersburg, Russia), 38, 93 bottom (Iraq Museum, Baghdad, Iraq), 64 (Lauros/Giraudon/Louvre, Paris, France), 16, 21 (Louvre, Paris, France/Giraudon), 30, 31 (National Museum, Damascus, Syria), 47 (Private Collection); Corbis Images: 59 (Archivo Iconografico, S.A.), 92, 96 (Bettmann), 44, 85, 90 bottom right (Gianni Dagli Orti), 67 (Todd A. Gipstein), 36, 37, 91 bottom (David Lees); Getty Images/Scott Peterson: 52, 86; Mary Evans Picture Library: 95 bottom; Stock Montage, Inc.: 28; Superstock, Inc.: 8, 90 top (Silvio Fiore/Museum of Baghdad, Baghdad, Iraq), 4, 18, 84 (Kurt Scholz); The Art Archive/Picture Desk: 58 top (British Museum), 6 (Dagli Orti), 43, 48, 90 bottom left (Dagli Orti/Archeological Museum of Bagdad), 32, 35, 62, 92 top left (Dagli Orti/British Museum), 12, 25 right, 33, 41, 91 top, 95 top (Dagli Orti/Musee du Louvre, Paris), 25 left (Dagli Orti/National Museum Damascus, Syria), 58 bottom (Eileen Tweedy/British Museum), 51; The Image Works: 15, 80, 93 top, 94 top (The British Museum/Topham-HIP), 26, 27 (Topham).

Cover art by Mike Jaroszko
Map by XNR Productions, Inc.

Library of Congress Cataloging-in-Publication Data

Schomp, Virginia.
Ancient Mesopotamia : the sumerians, babylonians, and assyrians / Virginia Schomp.
p. cm. — (People of the ancient world)
Includes bibliographical references and index.
ISBN 0-531-11818-5 (lib. bdg.) 0-531-16741-0 (pbk.)
1. Iraq—Civilization—To 634—Juvenile literature. I. Title. II. Series.
DS69.5.S44 2004
935—dc22

2004001947

Printed in the United States of America.
1 2 3 4 5 6 7 8 9 10 R 13 12 11 10 09 08 07 06 05 04

Contents

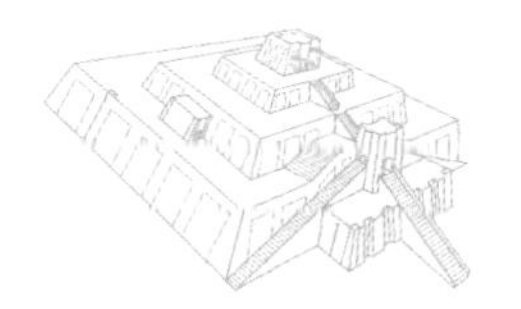

CRADLE OF CIVILIZATION

For centuries the ancient civilizations of Mesopotamia lay buried under mounds of dirt. Then, in the mid-1800s, travelers from Europe began to dig up the past. Some came to the deserts of the Middle East seeking works of art to display in museums. Others hoped to find proof that Bible stories set in the region were true. Still others were searching for evidence of how people lived long ago. In their quest for knowledge and treasure, these explorers uncovered long-lost cities, temples, libraries, and palaces. Their discoveries shed light not just on Mesopotamia's past but on the very beginnings of history.

The historic region of Mesopotamia lay between the Tigris and Euphrates Rivers, in roughly the same place as modern-day Iraq. The ancient Greeks gave the region its name, which means "land between the rivers." Mesopotamia was part of a larger arc of land known as the **Fertile Crescent.** Extending from the eastern shore of the Mediterranean Sea all the way to the Persian Gulf, the Fertile Crescent was home to some of the world's earliest farmers.

The people of ancient Mesopotamia depended on the waters of the Tigris and Euphrates Rivers. This is a view of the Euphrates River today.

The first farming villages appeared in the northern foothills of the Fertile Crescent around 9000 B.C. Centuries later, some of the

farmers moved south. They found a broad plain of dry but rich soil stretching between the Tigris and Euphrates Rivers. By digging canals to channel water from the rivers and **irrigate** their fields, the settlers raised abundant crops. Their population grew. Small villages developed into thriving towns. Around 3500 B.C., in an area of southern Mesopotamia known as Sumer, these pioneers laid the foundations of the first civilization.

The Sumerians built the world's first cities. They invented the first practical system of writing. They developed organized government, religion, and law. They also made remarkable advances in science, technology, and mathematics. For their many accomplishments, Mesopotamia is known as the "cradle of civilization."

Around 2000 B.C., Sumer fell to foreign conquerors. Over the centuries that followed, a series of mighty empires ruled the land between the rivers. These included two of the ancient world's greatest civilizations, Babylonia and Assyria. Altogether, the civilizations of Mesopotamia dominated the Middle East for nearly three thousand years. Their glory and achievements influenced nearly every other ancient culture and helped shape our modern world.

Today historians must dig deep to gather information about ancient Mesopotamia. The people of the region's great civilizations did not leave behind massive stone temples or monuments. Instead, they built mainly with mud bricks. Over time even their grandest structures crumbled. Mounds of earth formed, and new buildings rose on top of the ruins. Through centuries of rebuilding, these mounds, or "**tells,**" climbed higher and higher.

Archaeologists carefully excavate the layers of the ancient tells. They study the ruined buildings, broken pottery, tools, weapons, household goods, and other **artifacts** recovered from the soil. Their most important finds have included hundreds of

Written records, such as the clay tablet shown here, have helped us understand the civilizations of ancient Mesopotamia.

thousands of clay tablets inscribed with government reports, laws, myths, prayers, business contracts, and personal letters. These were the world's first written records. The wealth of information they contain has helped archaeologists piece together a picture of what life was like in ancient Mesopotamia.

Leonard Woolley, one of the best-known excavators of Sumer, wrote that the mission of archaeology is to "breathe life" into the "dry bones" of history. By uncovering long-buried places and deciphering long-lost writings, archaeologists bring alive the people who lived in ancient Mesopotamia. Their discoveries also take us to the roots of some of our most basic beliefs, institutions, and technologies. As Woolley described it, beneath the mounds of earth dotting historic Mesopotamia, we meet our "spiritual forebears [ancestors]. . . . Almost every object found is not merely an illustration of the achievements of a particular race at a particular time, but also a . . . picture of the beginnings [of] our modern world."

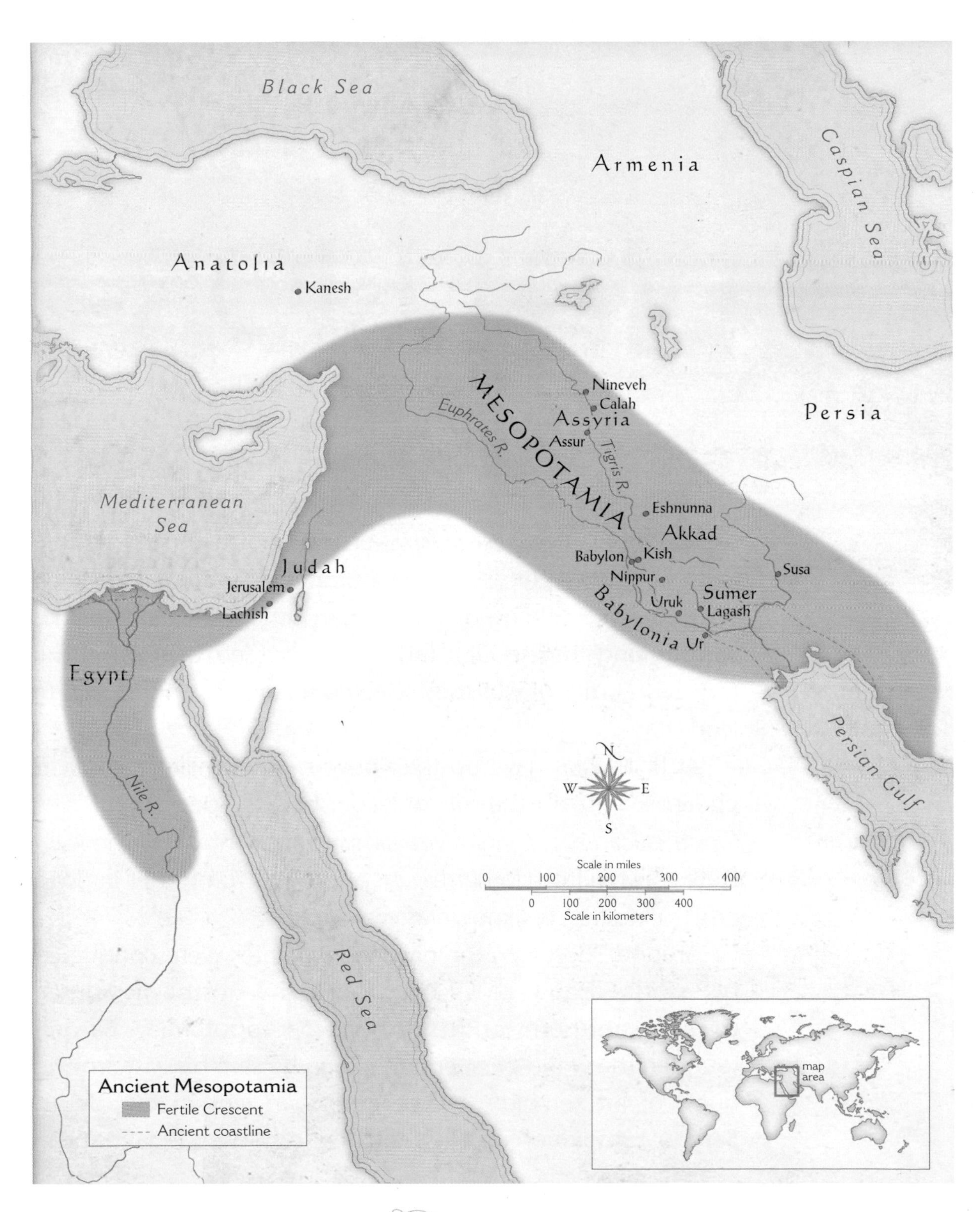
Black Sea
Armenia
Caspian Sea
Anatolia
Kanesh
MESOPOTAMIA
Nineveh
Calah
Assyria
Assur
Euphrates R.
Tigris R.
Persia
Mediterranean Sea
Eshnunna
Akkad
Babylon
Kish
Nippur
Susa
Judah
Jerusalem
Lachish
Sumer
Uruk
Lagash
Babylonia
Ur
Egypt
Persian Gulf
Nile R.
N
W
E
S
Scale in miles
0
100
200
300
400
0
100
200
300
400
Scale in kilometers
Red Sea
map area
Ancient Mesopotamia
Fertile Crescent
Ancient coastline

THE WARRIOR-KINGS

Mesopotamia's earliest civilization was not a unified nation. Instead, Sumer consisted of a number of independent city-states, each including a large city and the farms and villages surrounding it. The city-states often battled over land and power. In times of war they selected a *lugal,* or "big man," to lead them.

At first *lugal*s gave up their power when military conflicts ended. Eventually the role of leader became permanent. The *lugal*s became the first-ever kings, and control of the city-states passed from father to son or brother to brother in powerful ruling families known as **dynasties.**

Around 2334 B.C., the divided city-states were conquered by King Sargon of Akkad, a region north of Sumer. Uniting northern and southern Mesopotamia, Sargon founded the world's first empire. Then he sent his vast army in quest of further glory. According to ancient **inscriptions,** Sargon's empire eventually stretched from the Mediterranean

The Sumerian King List

Archaeologists exploring the buried ruins of Mesopotamia have found more than twenty different copies of the Sumerian King List. First inscribed in clay nearly four thousand years ago, this ancient text names the kings of Sumer, dynasty by dynasty. It is a mixture of fact and legend.

"After the kingship descended from heaven," the text begins, "Alulim became king. He ruled for 28,800 years." Other legendary kings had equally fantastic reigns. In fact, the list names only eight kings for the first 241,200 years of Sumerian history.

Later kings had more reasonable histories. Archaeologists have discovered other ancient records confirming that many of these rulers were real people. They included "Ku-Bau, the innkeeper, she who made firm the foundations of Kish." Ku-Bau was the only known woman "king" of a Sumerian city-state.

This nearly complete copy of the Sumerian King List was written around 2125 B.C.

Sea to the Persian Gulf, making him master of all lands "from the sunrise to the sunset."

After Sargon's death his empire fell apart. Again the warrior-kings of Sumer battled for supremacy. Meanwhile, forces were rising that would take Mesopotamia to new heights of power and glory.

Hammurabi was a Babylonian king who is remembered mainly for his famous code of laws.

Babylonia and Assyria

In 1792 B.C., Hammurabi took the throne of the city-state of Babylon. Driven by dreams of empire, this warrior-king attacked and overcame all rivals. At last he succeeded in turning his small city into the capital of a reunited Mesopotamia. To mark his triumphs, Hammurabi erected stone pillars proclaiming himself "the sun of Babylon, who causes light to go forth over the lands of Sumer and Akkad, the king who has made the four quarters of the world subservient [submissive]."

The kings who followed Hammurabi gradually lost control of the Babylonian Empire. For centuries, Mesopotamia was torn by conflict and invasion. During these troubled times, the northern kingdom of Assyria began to build its own empire.

Accounts in the Bible and in ancient Babylonian chronicles portray the Assyrians as fierce, bloodthirsty conquerors. After crushing an enemy, an Assyrian king would execute or mutilate hundreds of captives. Here is how King Assurnasirpal II described his treatment of the people of one rebellious city:

> I captured many troops alive. I cut off of some their arms and hands; I cut off of others their noses, ears, and extremities. I gouged out the eyes of many troops. I made one pile of the living and one of the heads. . . . I burnt their adolescent boys and girls.

By the seventh century B.C., the dreaded Assyrian armies had seized lands stretching from Egypt to Persia (present-day Iran). It was the largest empire the world had ever seen. Assurbanipal, one of the Assyrian Empire's last rulers, proclaimed himself "king of the universe, [who] has brought into submission at his feet all princes."

Assurbanipal commemorated his triumphs in **reliefs** (sculptures that stand out from a flat background) on the walls of his palace at Nineveh. Unearthed from the ruins, his sculptures depict a ruler who was both a merciless tyrant and a cultured scholar. In one scene the king reclines in his elegant garden, enjoying a bowl of wine, while the head of a vanquished rival dangles from a nearby tree.

Soon after Assurbanipal's death in 627 B.C., widespread revolts toppled the Assyrian Empire. For a brief time Babylonia regained its former glory. The outstanding ruler of the New Babylonian Empire was Nebuchadrezzar II.

The Bible portrays Nebuchadrezzar as the ruthless oppressor who destroyed Jerusalem in 586 B.C. and carried the Hebrew people into exile. Babylonian histories celebrate him as the tireless builder who restored the city of Babylon. He rebuilt the capital's walls, temples, and palaces, and he encouraged art and learning. Under his rule Babylon became one of the ancient world's most dazzling centers of power, wealth, and culture.

Royal Responsibilities

Nebuchadrezzar ruled during Mesopotamia's final burst of glory. The traditions of his rule got their start centuries earlier, with the first kings of Sumer, and persisted through thousands of years of imperial history.

The citizens of Sumer, Babylonia, and Assyria believed that their kings were extraordinary mortals, chosen by the gods to serve as their representatives on earth. That exalted role brought many important responsibilities.

First, the king was the chief priest of the state religion. He was responsible for building temples and performing rituals to ensure the blessings of Mesopotamia's many gods. Ancient sculptures often show kings molding the first brick or carrying the first basket of earth for the construction of a splendid new temple. Rulers often stamped their names in the bricks of the temple to make sure the gods remembered their contributions.

Equally sacred was the king's duty to protect and extend his domain. He maintained the capital's defensive walls. He raised troops and personally led them into battle. His conquests glorified the gods and brought the empire treasure and greater security.

Kings also had an obligation to ensure the well-being of their subjects. This included maintaining and improving the all-important irrigation canals and keeping the roads in good repair. Most importantly, it meant promoting law and justice. Hammurabi, founder of the Babylonian Empire, set down one of the ancient world's most famous codes of law. In his opening to the Code of Hammurabi, the king maintained that the gods had called him "to make justice appear in the land, to destroy the evil and the wicked that the strong might not oppress the weak, to rise like the sun-god . . . to give light to the land."

Assyrian king Assurbanipal carries a basket of earth. The inscription on the stone proclaims that the king restored a shrine to Ea, god of fresh water and wisdom.

The Code of Hammurabi

In 1901 archaeologists discovered a tall black pillar buried near the ancient city of Susa, in present-day Iran. Engraved on the stone were 282 laws set down by Hammurabi of Babylon. Hammurabi's code of laws called for severe penalties for crime, as well as protection for the helpless. Here are a few examples:

> If anyone is committing a robbery and is caught, then he shall be put to death.
>
> If a man put out the eye of another man, his eye shall be put out.
>
> If a son strikes his father, his hands shall be hewn off.
>
> If a man takes a wife, and she be seized by disease, . . . he shall keep her in the house which he has built and support her so long as she lives.

The most complete source of Hammurabi's code of laws is this engraved stone pillar discovered in Iran. The engraving at the top shows the king standing before Shamash, god of law and justice.

Life at Court

Along with its many duties, the role of king also brought great power and privilege. Discoveries made in buried palaces give us a glimpse of the luxurious life at court.

The royal palace was a huge collection of buildings sprawled over many acres. There were temples, workshops, storerooms, a throne room, a reception hall, private apartments for the ruler and his family, and quarters for officials and servants. Nestled among all these structures were gardens, paved walkways, and courtyards. Thick earthen walls studded with watchtowers surrounded the entire complex.

Palace records show that kings spent much of their time in the throne room, attending to government business. Seated on a raised platform, surrounded by guards and attendants, the ruler received ambassadors bearing **tribute** from foreign courts. He listened to government officials report on affairs throughout the kingdom. He granted audience to a stream of important citizens, who knelt before the throne to deliver their petitions. These requests might include a decision in a legal matter, forgiveness of debts, or help in recovering a runaway wife.

When the king's work was finished, he enjoyed the finest foods and wines at his daily banquet. Sometimes family members joined him at the feast. The royal household often included the king's children, nephews, and cousins. He had one legal wife, the queen. Most rulers also had a number of lower-ranking wives, or **concubines.** The ladies of the court had special quarters that were separate from the rest of the palace. Although they lived in great luxury, few royal women had any political power or influence.

A favorite royal pastime was hunting for wild animals. Both sport and ritual, the hunt represented the ruler's role as defender

The Beasts of Nimrud

In the ninth century B.C., Assyrian king Assurnasirpal II celebrated the completion of his palace at Calah (present-day Nimrud, Iraq) with an enormous banquet. For ten days, according to inscriptions carved in the palace walls, "69,574 invited guests" enjoyed a menu including "1,000 fattened head of cattle, 1,000 calves, 10,000 stable sheep, . . . 10,000 jars of beer, [and] 10,000 skins of wine." Watching over the festivities were "beasts of the mountains" carved from "white limestone and alabaster."

In 1846 British archaeologist Henry Layard discovered the colossal statue of a fierce man-headed beast in the palace ruins. According to his account, one of his workmen was so terrified "on catching the first glimpse of the monster" that he ran off "as fast as his legs could carry him."

Colossal man-headed beasts guarded the palace of Assurnasirpal in Nimrud.

of the empire against the forces of evil. The wall sculptures at Nineveh show King Assurbanipal hunting lions in his personal game park. "On the plain savage lions, fierce creatures of the mountains, rose against me," proclaims the king's inscription. "I seized a fierce lion of the plain by his ears. . . . I pierced his body with my lance. . . . Upon the lions which I slew, I rested the fierce bow of the goddess Ishtar."

NOBLES, GOVERNMENT OFFICIALS, AND PRIESTS

The king stood at the top of ancient Mesopotamian society. Beneath him were the wealthy landowners who made up the small but powerful upper class. These nobles included princes and other royal relatives, as well as leading military officers, government officials, and priests.

The most important noble was the **crown prince,** usually the ruler's oldest son. He sometimes had his own separate palace, where he studied the arts of governing and waging war. The king often made his other male relatives governors of conquered territories. One of his daughters was appointed high priestess of Inanna, goddess of love and war. His other daughters might be married off to foreign rulers to cement alliances.

The crown prince spent much of his time preparing for the responsibilities of kingship. This statue of Gudea, a Sumerian prince, was made around 2150 B.C.

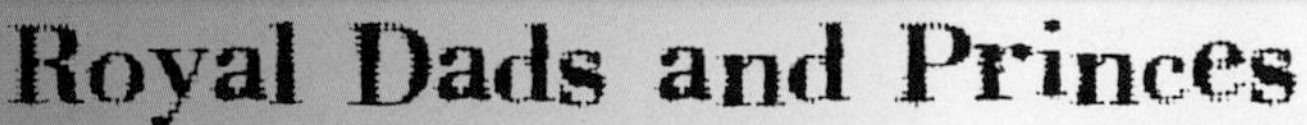

Royal Dads and Princes

Like all fathers and sons, Mesopotamian kings and princes sometimes quarreled. Clay tablets found in the city-state of Mari record disagreements between Assyrian governor Yasmah-Adad and his father, King Shamshi-Adad I. In one letter the king compared Yasmah-Adad to his more successful older brother. The unhappy prince sent this reply:

> I read the letter that you sent me, Daddy, in which you said: *How much longer must we keep you on a leading rein? Don't you see that your brother is directing vast armies? You just direct your own palace!* Now how can I be like a child and incapable of directing affairs when Daddy promoted me? How can it be that . . . some servant or other has succeeded in ousting me from my Daddy's affections?

Arms of the Government

In addition to their royal relatives, Mesopotamia's rulers relied on a network of government officials to manage their far-flung lands. Filling the ranks of this vast **bureaucracy** were district chiefs, town mayors, tax collectors, clerks, and many other officeholders. Most high-ranking bureaucrats were appointed by the king. Sometimes a government post became hereditary and was passed down from father to son.

One important arm of government was the citizen's council. Local councils usually included the mayor and leading citizens of a city or village. In Sumerian times councils met to discuss and resolve problems in the community. In at least one case, an assembly elected a king. According to ancient inscriptions, after the people of the Sumerian city-state of Kish overthrew an unpopular ruler, the citizens "assembled . . . and raised Iphur-Kishi, the man of Kish, . . . to kingship."

By early Babylonian times, councils had lost their political power. However, they still played an important role in settling legal disputes. Men and women argued their cases before the local council. After considering the facts, the members of the council announced their decision.

Citizens who were dissatisfied with the council's decision could ask for a hearing before a higher court of professional judges. After the trial a clerk inscribed a record of the proceedings on a soft clay tablet. Archaeologists have uncovered thousands of these ancient court documents. They show that the Mesopotamians conducted their trials in a way that would seem familiar to us today.

At the opening of a trial, the judges made all parties swear to tell the truth, usually while touching a symbol of the gods, such as "the divine Spear-symbol of Ishtar." Then they listened to testimony from people on both sides of the argument. They called in witnesses and examined the evidence. Finally they pronounced judgment. The judges' ruling often included an explanation of how they had reached their verdict. One court found a man guilty "because the witnesses contradicted his statement and demonstrated him to be a criminal." Even that was not the final word. Citizens could appeal the higher court's decisions all the way to the king, the ultimate legal authority.

An unusual feature of Mesopotamian justice was the River Ordeal. When judges could not decide who was telling the truth in a serious case such as a murder trial, they might order the accused to jump into the river. If he was innocent, he survived. If he was guilty, the gods made sure that he drowned, taking care of both the verdict and the punishment.

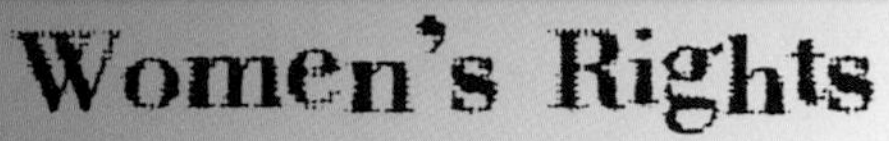

Women's Rights

Although Mesopotamian women could appear in court, they did not have the same legal rights as men. In Assyrian times especially, the laws made the husband the undisputed head of the household. Archaeologists excavating the ruins of the Assyrian city of Assur found clay tablets containing laws relating to women. The tablets outlined harsh punishments for married women who committed a variety of offenses, from appearing in public without a veil to asking their husbands for a divorce. Women's status was summed up in a final clause: "Apart from the penalties for a married woman which are written on the tablet, a man may flog his wife, he may pull out her hair, he may damage and split her ears. There is nothing wrong in this."

Gods and Demons

The people of Mesopotamia believed in thousands of different gods. Chief among these were An, god of the heavens; Enlil, god of the air; Enki, god of the waters; and Ishtar (also called Inanna), goddess of love and war. In Babylonian times, Marduk became "director of all the gods." The Assyrians gave that exalted role to their national god, Assur.

Besides these chief gods, the spirit world included many lesser deities. There were gods of the sun, the moon, grain, the pickax, and nearly every other aspect of heaven and earth. A host of "personal gods" helped and guided individuals. Dangerous ghosts and demons brought evils such as sickness and sandstorms.

After death, a person's body and soul traveled to the "land of no return." This dark and gloomy afterworld was ruled by Ereshkigal, goddess of the dead. Families buried their loved ones with as many personal possessions as they could afford, from a few

Ishtar, goddess of love and war, is represented in a third-century B.C. sculpture. The horned dragon representing the Babylonian god Marduk was made in the sixth century B.C.

simple pots and beads for poor peasants to lavish jewelry and other luxuries for the wealthy. In early Sumerian times kings and queens sometimes went to their graves accompanied by attendants who were sacrificed to serve them in the next world.

Archaeologists have found extensive evidence of the Mesopotamians' vast and complex belief system. The ruins of palace libraries often contain long lists of the gods, which were prepared for use in schools. Other clay tablets immortalized the gods in myths, hymns, and prayers. These ancient texts reveal a very close relationship between the people of Mesopotamia and their gods. Here is part of a Sumerian text describing a man's prayer to his personal god and the divine being's answer:

> There is a young man who spends the time in grief, illness and bitter suffering. Before his god the youth weeps bitterly. "My god, the day shines bright over the Land, but for me the day is black. My god, you who are my father who begot me, lift up my face." The man's god heard his bitter weeping. He scattered to the winds the grief which had spread its arms round him. He turned the young man's suffering into joy.

The Holy Estate

The center of every Mesopotamian city was the temple. This holy estate was not only a house of worship but also an economic and political power.

The first temples were small mud-brick structures built on low platforms to raise them above flood levels. Over time that simple design grew into the majestic pyramid-shaped temple-towers known as **ziggurats**. The ziggurat had several stepped platforms, connected by outside staircases, and a shrine or temple at the top. The city's **patron god** lived in the temple's inner sanctuary in the form of a statue.

The ziggurat of Ur was dedicated to the goddess Inanna around 2100 B.C. The ancient Mesopotamians built temples like this from hundreds of thousands of mud bricks.

The Tower of Babel

Mesopotamia's most famous ziggurat stood in Babylon. First built by Hammurabi nearly four thousand years ago, this temple inspired the story of the Tower of Babel. According to the Bible, when men tried to build "a tower with its top in the heavens," God halted the project by making the workers speak in different tongues.

Over time Hammurabi's temple crumbled. In the sixth century B.C., Nebuchadrezzar completed a glorious restoration. Soaring 300 feet (90 meters) into the air, this eight-story ziggurat was one of the wonders of the ancient world.

In modern times many travelers searched for Nebuchadrezzar's temple. Finally, in the early 1900s, German archaeologist Robert Koldewey identified the site. All that remained was a waterlogged ditch tracing the huge square foundation of the lost Tower of Babel.

This is how one modern-day artist pictured the lost Tower of Babel.

Surrounding the temple was a large complex of buildings. There were workshops in which craftspeople turned out a variety of goods to be used in the temple or sold. Storerooms and granaries held produce from the temple's farms, orchards, and fisheries. Offices and living quarters accommodated the large staff of priests who managed the god's estate. Most temple personnel were men. There were a few separate communities of priestesses. These were mainly women from upper-class families who had been sent by their families to spend their days praying for their loved ones back home.

With the wealth that came from all its properties, the temple provided a variety of community services. It granted loans without interest to citizens in need. It took in orphans and children from poor families. The temple staff also worked closely with the king, guiding his performance of his religious duties and watching for evil **omens.**

Omens were signs of the gods' intentions. They could be found just about anywhere—in thunder, earthquakes, or markings on the liver of a sacrificial lamb. Priests advised one Assyrian king who was troubled by ill omens to recite certain spells for protection. As part of the "prescription," the ruler was told to "put on the loose robe of a nurse [and] go down to the river to wash himself."

Servants to the Gods

Most priests worked at jobs related to the temple's business affairs. They might supervise the workshops or record gifts sent by wealthy citizens. The greatest responsibility of the temple staff, however, was taking care of the gods' needs.

The Mesopotamians believed that, in many ways, gods were very much like people. They needed food and a place to live.

Priests prepare to honor the gods with an animal sacrifice.

They felt love, anger, and other human emotions. When their needs were fulfilled, they were content, and they blessed the land with prosperity. When the gods were neglected, disasters such as floods, drought, or disease could follow.

To keep the gods happy, priests conducted a daily round of

rituals, prayers, and sacrifices. Most importantly, they cared for the temple's divine image. Attendants bathed and dressed this precious wooden statue and entertained it with soothing music. According to clay tablets found in the ruins of a Sumerian temple, they also served it two meals a day. Each morning and evening the priests set up tables in the inner sanctuary and heaped them with meats, fruits, and beverages. Gods apparently had a powerful appetite. One text listed a daily menu including more than forty sheep, eight lambs, seventy birds and ducks, and fifty-four containers of wine and beer. The "leftovers" were sent to the king's table or used to feed the temple staff and their families.

Priests performed most of their holy work behind the temple walls. On special occasions the whole community joined in worship. The most elaborate Babylonian religious celebration was the New Year's festival. This grand event featured sacred ceremonies and recitals of religious stories. The highlight was a colorful parade through the streets of Babylon. Jeweled chariots carried the images of Marduk, Ishtar, and "visiting gods" from other cities. Leading the way was the king. "The Lord of Babylon goes forth," he proclaimed at the start of the procession. "The lands kneel before him. Ishtar goes forth, aromatic herbs burn with fragrance. By the side of Ishtar of Babylon, while her servants play the flute, Goes all Babylon exultant."

MERCHANTS AND TRADERS

Mesopotamia's great civilizations could not have developed without foreign trade. The land between the rivers had fertile soil for farming but almost no timber, stone, or metal. Cities imported these goods by land and water. Managing that vital business was the job of an enterprising band of merchant-traders.

Merchants were part of the broad middle class that included the bulk of Mesopotamian society. The lines between the social classes were not permanently fixed. Merchants who were very capable or lucky in business could rise to the ranks of the wealthy landowners. On the other hand, bad business deals could sink an unlucky merchant to the lowly status of a slave.

A Vast Trading Network

Around 1900 B.C., an Assyrian merchant sent a clay tablet to his representative in Kanesh, a city in **Anatolia** (modern-day

Turkey). "The guards are strong," the merchant's letter warned. "Lookouts have been appointed." It seems that the king of Assur was cracking down on merchants who dealt in restricted goods, such as luxury items reserved for the nobility. Palace guards had just jailed a trader who was caught receiving a shipment of prohibited merchandise. "Please," the merchant begged his associate, "do not smuggle anything."

The clay tablets discovered at Kanesh provide evidence of

Ancient Mesopotamian traders used ships to carry all sorts of goods. This relief shows Assyrian merchants transporting a cargo of wood.

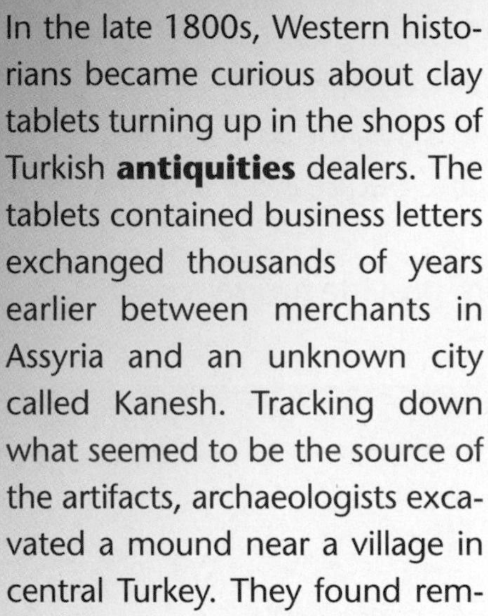

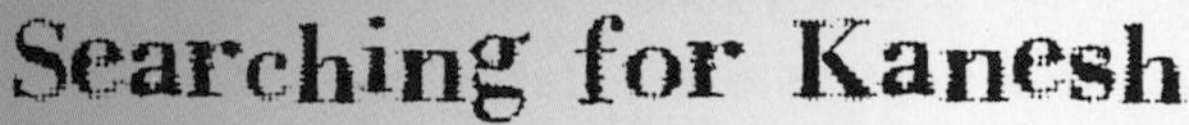

Searching for Kanesh

In the late 1800s, Western historians became curious about clay tablets turning up in the shops of Turkish **antiquities** dealers. The tablets contained business letters exchanged thousands of years earlier between merchants in Assyria and an unknown city called Kanesh. Tracking down what seemed to be the source of the artifacts, archaeologists excavated a mound near a village in central Turkey. They found remnants of ancient buildings but no tablets. Then, in 1925, a local man led searchers to a spot just north of the village. Soon the archaeologists uncovered the ruins of an ancient Assyrian trading colony on the outskirts of Kanesh. More than sixteen thousand tablets were eventually recovered. These ancient records provided a wealth of information on Mesopotamia's merchant-traders.

extensive and profitable business dealings between Assyria and the people of Anatolia. This was just one branch of a vast trading network that flourished for thousands of years, taking Mesopotamian merchants to the far corners of their known world.

Trading ships sailed the Red Sea, the Mediterranean Sea, and the Persian Gulf. **Caravans** traveled along extensive overland trade routes. Ancient account books list the merchandise exported from Mesopotamia, mostly grain and cloth. In exchange, merchant-traders brought home both practical goods and luxury items. These included lead, silver, gold, pine, cedar, cypress, pearls, semiprecious stones, spices, and perfumes.

Overland Trade

Mesopotamia's traveling merchants carried their goods overland in trading caravans. Their sturdy donkeys plodded over rough paths, carrying merchandise on their backs and in bulging side packs. Trade routes often crossed desolate deserts and rugged mountains. The travelers faced severe heat and cold, hungry wolves, and the constant threat of bandits. After a journey of many weeks or months, they finally reached their destination.

For Assyrian caravans, the end of the line was usually a colony of fellow traders. These "middlemen" settled abroad to handle the distribution of trade goods sent by their associates back

An Assyrian relief found in Nineveh shows Assyrian traders traveling in a caravan.

home. The merchants in the trading colony at Kanesh received textiles and tin, which they exchanged throughout Anatolia for gold and silver. Caravans then carried the payments back to Assur. One letter from an Assyrian merchant to his partner in Kanesh contained a detailed inventory of a shipment that included "2 fine textiles, 1 garment, . . . 2 head-scarves, 32 1/2 **minas** of tin [and] 2 black donkeys. . . . All this [the caravan] is bringing you. Sell it at the best price and send me the silver."

Archaeologists have excavated large areas of Ur, including the ziggurat, marketplace, and streets lined with houses.

Merchants paid taxes to local rulers at both ends of the trade route and often at several towns in between. They also had to deal with frequent political upheavals, which could make trade difficult or impossible. One Assyrian merchant sent this reply to a business partner's request for merchandise from Akkad: "Since you left, the Akkadians have not entered the City. Their country is in revolt. If they arrive before winter, and there is the possibility of a purchase which allows you profit, we will buy for you."

Despite all the costs and difficulties, fortunes could be made through trade. While most members of the middle class lived in humble one-story brick homes, merchant-traders often enjoyed more lavish dwellings. Archaeologists excavating the Sumerian city-state of Ur found the remains of two-story homes owned by prosperous merchants. Many of these comfortable town houses had a brick-paved courtyard, a chapel, a private bedroom, guest rooms, a bathroom, and quarters for several servants or slaves.

Buyers and Sellers

While traders reached out to the far corners of the known world, other merchants operated on a far smaller scale. Peddlers such as

The Splendors of Babylon

Mesopotamia's cities were bustling centers of business, trade, politics, religion, and culture. Most splendid of all was Babylon. Massive walls surrounded this glorious capital. Guarding the main entrance was the Ishtar Gate. In an inscription on the walls of that immense gate, King Nebuchadrezzar declared, "I placed wild bulls and ferocious dragons in the gateway . . . so that mankind might gaze on them in wonder."

In 1899, German archaeologists began excavating the mounds of Babylon. They found thousands of fragments of glazed bricks from the shattered gate. As they fitted the pieces together, brightly colored relief images of bulls and dragons appeared. After thirty-one years of painstaking labor, the Ishtar Gate stood again, in a specially built hall inside a German museum.

The beautifully decorated Ishtar Gate guarded the main entrance to Babylon. It was completely covered with colorful glazed bricks.

the "firewood man" and the "salt man" sold their goods door-to-door. Shopkeepers in large cities sold merchandise to individuals in busy "market streets," or bazaars.

When British archaeologist Leonard Woolley excavated a bazaar in Ur, he found a maze of narrow streets that reminded him of many modern-day Middle Eastern markets. Visitors to this noisy, bustling quarter could choose from booths stocked with fresh fruits and vegetables, chickens, ducks, dried fish, cheese, and spices. There were also displays of clothing, pottery, and other local craftwork. Wealthier shoppers might buy imported luxuries such as fine linen from Egypt, ivory hair combs from Persia, and pearls from the Red Sea.

Purchases were usually paid for in units of grain or silver. Wise shoppers kept a close eye on the merchant weighing out their order. One ancient tablet complained about a dishonest shopkeeper who "as he holds the balance, indulges in cheating by substituting weights."

Accounting tablets from Sumerian cities show that merchants also used a system based on silver to keep track of their income and expenses. The merchant listed all the goods he had purchased in the past year, alongside those he had received as payment. Next to each item he noted its value in units of silver. Subtracting expenses from income told the merchant how much money he had made or lost.

Losses could be more than a business problem. For some merchant-traders, they were a personal disaster. To fund big trading ventures, merchants often took out loans from wealthy citizens who set themselves up as bankers. If the borrower was unable to repay the loan and interest, he might lose his estate. Sometimes his children, or even his entire family, were sold into slavery to pay his debts.

ARTISANS AND ARTISTS

Mesopotamia's artisans produced the practical objects that were the foundation of their civilization, such as tablets for writers, weapons for warriors, and tools for farmers and builders. Artists created treasures to glorify the kings and gods. Often the line between artisan and artist blurred, as skill and creativity turned even everyday objects into works of art.

Most craftspeople worked in large temple or palace workshops. Business records from the workshop of one Sumerian temple listed specialists in many departments, including leatherworkers, metalworkers, stonecutters, goldsmiths, and carpenters. Large cities also had a number of private workshops. Shops practicing the same craft may have clustered together on the same streets. Archaeologists have excavated city quarters covered in debris from pottery production and from the working of gems and shells.

Knowledge of crafts was usually passed down orally, from father to son. Occasionally craftspeople wrote down detailed information such as formulas. Their manuals were strictly for

A terra-cotta plaque shows a Babylonian carpenter at work.

the eyes of "initiates," those admitted to the artisans' ranks. One craft manual opened with a warning: "Let the initiate show the initiate; the non-initiate shall not see it. It belongs to the tabooed [prohibited] things of the great gods."

Crafting Nature's Bounty

Most Mesopotamian artisans worked with readily available materials. The most common craft material was clay. Potters turned wet clay into handsome pots, plates, bowls, and jars. Other clay workers made the bricks used for houses and monumental building projects and the tablets that preserved the story of their civilization.

Basket makers worked with the reeds that flourished in the marshlands and along the rivers. They wove a variety of useful objects, including baskets, mats, furniture, and small boats. Leatherworkers tanned the hides of farm animals to produce harnesses, shoes, sandals, and bags.

Palace and temple workshops often employed thousands of textile workers, mostly women. Some spun sheep's wool into thread. Some wove the thread on looms to make cloth. Women also engaged in spinning and weaving at home, making clothing for their families or earning extra income. An eighth-century B.C. temple relief shows a noblewoman spinning thread while a servant keeps her cool with a fan.

Glassmaking was another important Mesopotamian craft. Artisans discovered how to make glass from a combination of sand and other ingredients some 3,300 years ago. Six centuries later, a glassmaker wrote down his "recipes." His tablet included detailed information on preparing, combining, and heating the ingredients, along with instructions for performing the proper religious offerings and sacrifices. "You first search in a favorable month for

A History in Clay

Pieces of pottery are usually the most common artifacts found at ancient sites. They can also be the most useful. At different times and places, people used different techniques to make pottery. The Mesopotamians shaped their first pots by hand around 8000 B.C., baking them at low temperatures to harden them. Thousands of years later, they developed the potter's wheel and more efficient pottery ovens. Shapes, colors, patterns, glazes, and other features also changed over time and place. By studying the pottery unearthed at a site, archaeologists can tell what groups of people lived there and when. Foreign-made vessels help them figure out trade links between civilizations. In these ways a simple pot or bowl can tell a story from the days before written history.

In ancient Mesopotamia spinning and weaving were usually considered "women's work." This relief shows a woman weaving thread on a loom.

a day of good omen," wrote the ancient artisan, "and only then can you set up the foundation of the furnace. . . . On the day when you plan to make glass, you make a sheep sacrifice. . . . Only then can you make the fire in the hearth of the furnace."

Treasures from Metal and Wood

Skilled artisans and artists also worked with materials that were in short supply in Mesopotamia and were therefore highly valued.

Carpenters made merchant ships, war chariots, and furniture for the temples and palaces. These artisans used fine imported woods such as cedar, walnut, and cypress. They filled out their work with lower-quality local timber, including mulberry and tamarisk. In the royal inscriptions unearthed at Nimrud, Assyrian king Assurnasirpal II boasted that he had built his palace "of cedar, cypress, juniper, boxwood, mulberry, pistachio-wood, and tamarisk, for my royal dwelling and for my lordly pleasure for all time."

Metalsmiths combined imported copper and tin to make bronze. The metal was melted at very high temperatures in special furnaces. Then it was poured into molds to make practical goods such as tools and weapons as well as luxury items, including vessels and statues. Sturdy tools and weapons were also made from iron.

Archaeologists have not found many metal artifacts in Mesopotamia. A discovery made in the mid-1800s helped explain why. In the ruins of an ancient workshop, excavators found a large stack of metal hoes, sickles, and other farm implements. The worn-out tools had been sent back from a temple at the end of the growing season so that the metal could be melted down and reused.

Jewelers worked with imported gold and silver, as well as semi-precious stones. These materials were crafted into exquisite earrings, bracelets, anklets, and other jewelry. Ancient texts describe the goddess Ishtar adorning herself: "Rings of gold I put on my hands, little stone beads I hung around my neck."

Mesopotamian artists also excelled in a technique called inlay. Fine wooden furniture, game boards, and musical instruments were inlaid with tiny bits of metal, glass, ivory, gems, and shells. The **mosaic** of carefully placed pieces formed a glittering design.

Ancient board games discovered in Ur are excellent examples of the craft of inlay. This game was made of wood inlaid with shell, red limestone, and lapis lazuli.

The Royal Graves of Ur

Much of our information about Mesopotamian jewelry comes from the royal graves of Ur. These Sumerian tombs date back to around 2700 B.C. In one grave archaeologists found the body of a queen named Puabi. She was wearing a fortune in jewelry, including gold earrings, pins, and rings. Her headdress was made from coils of gold ribbons topped with gold leaves and flowers.

The tombs also held a grim surprise. Hundreds of attendants had been sacrificed to serve their ruler in the afterworld. The bodies of the serving women lay in neat rows. They were adorned in headdresses, earrings, and necklaces made of gold, silver, and semiprecious stones. They seemed to have died peacefully, probably from drinking poison.

Historians have reconstructed the gold and lapis lazuli headdress of Queen Puabi.

Masterpieces in Stone

Some of Mesopotamia's greatest artistic treasures were carved from stone. Stone statues and reliefs adorned temples and palaces. Reliefs were often commissioned by kings to glorify their victories on the battlefield and at the hunt. These sculptures were carved on huge slabs of stone, which were placed against the mud-brick palace walls.

Another type of stone art was meant for ordinary citizens. The people of Mesopotamia believed that it was essential to show constant devotion to the gods. Because it was impossible to pray all the time, they hired sculptors to make small stone "praying statues," which they placed in the temple as their stand-ins. Archaeologists discovered a collection of these statues in the ruins of a temple in Eshnunna, near present-day Baghdad. The appealing figurines have huge eyes that are turned up to heaven, and their hands are clasped in eternal prayer.

Sculptors also expressed their creativity in an even smaller art form, the cylinder seal. Like official stamps or signatures, cylinder

Four ancient cylinder seals are shown next to their impressions in clay. The seal impressions depict scenes from the *Epic of Gilgamesh* (see page 82).

seals were used to mark personal property and to seal legal documents. A scene or design was carved into a small cylinder of stone, ivory, or some other hard material. When the seal was rolled over soft clay, it created a continuous pattern.

Seal makers used drills and engraving tools to carve a variety of intricate designs: plants and animals, kings and heroes, scenes from hunting, battle, and mythology. Many of their creations were tiny masterpieces, full of life and movement. Cylinder seals are also a valuable source of historical information, recording milestones such as the invention of the arch and dome in architecture. The inscriptions tell us about the seal owner's personal history and beliefs. One fourteenth-century B.C. seal carried this appeal to the owner's personal god: "Sublime lord, prince in whose hands the power of decision in heaven and on earth has been vested; the servant who worships you, by your look may he be happy."

PEASANT FARMERS

The great majority of Mesopotamians were farmers. The rest of society, from artisans and merchants to priests and kings, depended on the produce from farm fields. According to a Sumerian legend, prosperity came to the land between the rivers when the gods "made the ewe give birth to the lamb [and] the grain increase in the furrows."

Despite their important work, farmers were near the bottom of the social ladder. Most free peasants farmed land owned by the temples, palaces, and nobles. Some hired themselves out to these estates as laborers, working for rations of food and wool. Some were tenant farmers who rented plots of land and paid for them with a portion of their harvests. Others owned their own small plots. These peasant landowners paid high taxes, usually in the form of government labor. Regardless of the arrangements, large landowners had all the advantages, and small farmers worked long and hard to scrape out a living.

Crops and Livestock

Most of what we know about the crops grown in ancient Mesopotamia comes from temple and palace records and

Mesopotamia's first farmers planted crops in the fertile plain between the Tigris and Euphrates Rivers. The riches of the region also included fish teeming in the rivers, swamps, and marshes.

The Agricultural Revolution

The people of Mesopotamia began to cultivate plants and herd animals sometime around 9000 B.C. They collected and planted seeds from naturally growing grains to produce a reliable food supply. They **domesticated** wild sheep, goats, boars, and cattle, providing themselves with "wealth on the hoof."

To trace this agricultural revolution, archaeologists study the remains of ancient plants and animal bones. They search for clues that help them tell the difference between wild and domesticated finds. For example, farmed wheat had firmer, easier-to-harvest ears than wild wheat, and domesticated animals had smaller bones than their wild relatives. Ancient artifacts also contain evidence. These sources include cylinder seals with images of farmers raising crops and tending the first domesticated animals.

from legal contracts between farmers and their employers. These documents show that the most important crops were **cereals** such as wheat and barley. Barley was used to make flour, porridge, and beer.

Vegetable crops included onions, garlic, leeks, peas, lentils, lettuce, and cucumbers. These were often planted in shade gardens. The growing plants were protected from the scorching sun and hot winds by tall date palm trees and smaller fruit trees, such as apple and pomegranate. One Sumerian myth tells the tale of a gardener who enjoyed a rich harvest of vegetables after the gods inspired him to plant in "the tree's protecting cover. . . . Its shade below, dawn, noon and dusk did not turn away."

Farmers and herders also raised livestock. Oxen pulled wagons and plows. Cows provided milk for butter and cheese, and their hides were tanned for leather. Shepherds tended huge flocks of goats and sheep. Raised mainly for their wool, sheep were so important that the Sumerians had more than two hundred words to describe all the different varieties.

Pairs of oxen pulled the plows on Mesopotamian farms. These useful animals also provided meat, and their hides were tanned to make leather.

The Farmer's Year

In 1950, American archaeologists uncovered a small clay tablet in the ancient city of Nippur. Inscribed around 1700 B.C., the document contained detailed instructions for running a family farm, written by a prosperous small farmer for his son. The "Farmer's Instructions" is the first known farming manual, as well as a valuable source of information on the Mesopotamian farmer's year.

The manual begins with the preparation of the fields in May or June. First, the farmer used irrigation waters to soften the parched ground. Once the field dried out, he worked the soil with hoes, using a hammer to "flatten the stubborn spots." Next, he plowed and planted. He took great care to use exactly the right amount of seed, based on a calculation of the number of furrows and the correct distance between seeds. The farmer advised his son to "keep your eye on the man who puts in the barley seed. Let him drop the grain uniformly two fingers deep."

When the seedlings began to sprout, the farmer offered prayers to Ninkilim, goddess of field mice and vermin, asking her to protect the growing grain. He followed a schedule of watering and weeding, and he watched for signs of disease. By early spring, nearly a year after planting, the crops were ready to be harvested. The manual cautioned the young farmer not to "let the barley bend over on itself" but to harvest it "in the day of its strength."

Seed was separated from the harvested plants with an ox-drawn threshing sledge. Prayers and rites were performed for "the grain not yet clean." Then the barley was tossed with pitchforks, which removed the chaff (seed coverings) and other debris. The farmer gave thanks for the harvest by "perform[ing] rites in the evening and at night."

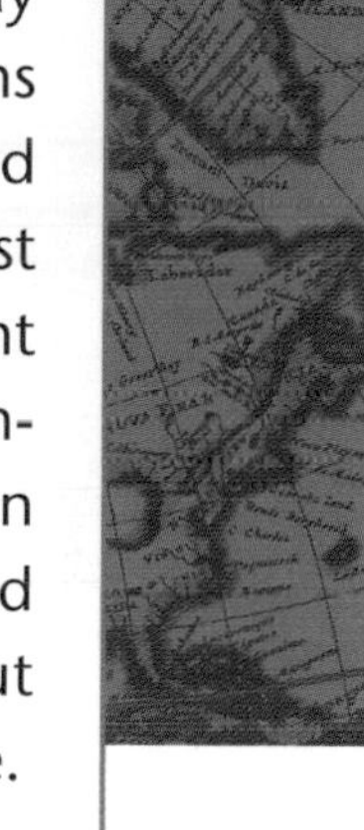

A Home Made from Reeds

Mesopotamian peasants who lived near marshes sometimes survived by fishing and catching wild birds instead of farming. These marsh dwellers built their homes from tall reeds. They set bundled reeds into the ground, then bent them and tied them together at the top. Sumerian stone carvings show the plumed tops of ancient reed houses.

Until recently, the people of the marshlands of southern Iraq lived much like these early Mesopotamians. Modern-day marsh dwellers fished in lagoons and trapped wild ducks and herons. They built reed huts just like those shown in the ancient carvings. Their way of life vanished in the early 1990s, when the Iraqi government drained the marshlands to drive out political opponents living there.

Troubles and Triumphs

When the spring floods were poor, crops failed. When river waters rose too high, not only fields of grain but entire villages could be lost. In addition, irrigation waters carried salts, which settled in the soil. Over time salted fields yielded fewer and fewer crops.

Farmers also had to contend with destructive sandstorms and sudden swarms of locusts. Lions and wolves carried off lambs. Diseases wiped out plants and livestock. In wartime, enemy armies trampled crops and drove off the farm animals. An ancient poem known as "Lamentation over the Destruction of Sumer and Ur" described the effects of a foreign invasion around 2000 B.C.: "Oxen no longer stand in their stalls. . . . Sheep no longer spread out in their sheepfold. . . . Rivers flow with bitter water. . . . Cultivated fields grow weeds."

In spite of all these dangers and uncertainties, Mesopotamia's farmers turned the dry land between the rivers into the ancient world's richest agricultural region. They accomplished this mainly through their sophisticated irrigation system. A series of large and small irrigation canals diverted river water to farm fields. The flow of the water was controlled by gates and other devices. Clay tablets record a Sumerian governor's construction of the first known canal around 2500 B.C.

Like the canal system, the Mesopotamian plow was a marvel of efficiency. Seeder plows not only turned the soil but also dropped seed through a funnel into the newly formed furrow. A cylinder seal from around 1300 B.C. shows a plow drawn by two oxen. The driver is holding a bag of seed to feed into the funnel.

Perhaps the farmer's most useful tool was the pickax. A type of short-handled hoe, this humble tool was put to work year-round. It was used for digging canals, building walls and houses, repairing streets, and preparing the soil for planting. According to a Sumerian poem, even the god Enlil "sang the praises of his pickax. . . . The pickax and the basket build cities. . . . The pickax is exalted."

SOLDIERS AND SLAVES

In many ways Mesopotamia's long history is a story of warfare. From the beginnings of civilization, the Sumerian city-states battled over boundaries and water rights. Kings raised large armies to fight off invaders and built their empires through conquest.

The first evidence of a standing (permanent) army comes from the reign of Sargon, around 2334 B.C. One of the king's inscriptions boasted that "5,400 warriors ate bread daily before him." Sargon used his powerful forces to "spread his terror-inspiring glamour over all the countries" and carve out the first Mesopotamian empire.

Masters of War

The Assyrians took warfare to new levels of terror and efficiency. Their highly disciplined army, composed of hundreds of thousands of troops, was one of the mightiest fighting forces of the ancient world. Assyrian soldiers excelled in both hand-to-hand combat and **siege** warfare. Reliefs show their highly effective

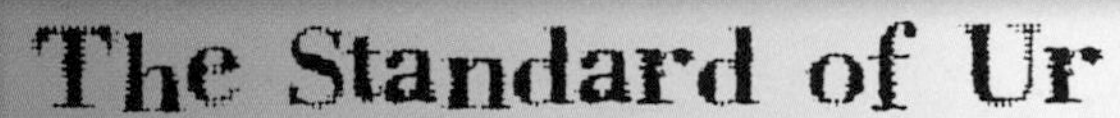

The Standard of Ur

One of the earliest illustrations of a Sumerian army is the Standard of Ur. Discovered in a royal tomb by archaeologist Leonard Woolley, this 4,500-year-old artifact consists of two panels inlaid with shell and **lapis lazuli,** fitted back to back in a wooden frame. One side shows peaceful Sumerians from all walks of life. On the other side soldiers are fighting a battle. **Infantrymen** march in formation, wearing long leather cloaks dotted with metal disks, possibly the world's first armor. Enemy soldiers are overrun by chariots, another Mesopotamian invention. In the final scene the army presents its prisoners to the triumphant king.

The Assyrians were known for their fierce and effective armies. This relief records Assurbanipal's conquest of a land in Arabia.

siege weapons, including iron-headed battering rams that were capable of smashing through stone and brick city walls.

In addition to direct combat, Assyrian rulers practiced what we might call "psychological warfare." When a king decided to invade a region, he first picked out one or two small, lightly defended cities. If the inhabitants refused to surrender, the army attacked, committing horrifying acts of murder and mutilation. Then the king publicized the atrocities in royal inscriptions and stone monuments to frighten the rest of the region into submission.

All Mesopotamian rulers claimed divine support for their military campaigns. In his royal inscriptions, Assyrian king Assurbanipal made this proud assertion:

> From my childhood, the great gods who dwell in Heaven and on Earth have granted me their favor. Like real fathers, they raised me, and instructed me in their exalted ways. They taught me to wage battle and combat, to give the signal for the skirmish and to draw up the line of battle. . . . They made my arms powerful against my foes.

In the Army

While many ancient texts and sculptures show Mesopotamia's armies at war, there is little information on exactly how those vast forces were raised. Some early Babylonian writings mention a government program called *ilkum.* Under the *ilkum* system men received a plot of land, which they paid for with a period of government service. They might spend a few months laboring on public projects, such as building temples or repairing canals, or they might serve in the army.

Assyrian armies were probably a mixture of draftees, professional soldiers, and captives from conquered territories who were pressed into service. The troops were led by the king and his generals. They were organized into several different units. Most prestigious was the elite force of charioteers. Assyria's swift

Substitute Soldiers

Some Mesopotamian men hired substitutes to take their place in the army. The Code of Hammurabi included strict laws regulating this practice. Under certain circumstances a man who had been "ordered to go upon the king's highway for war" was permitted to send a mercenary (hired soldier) in his place. However, if he withheld his substitute's pay, he would be "put to death, and he who represented him shall take possession of his house."

horse-drawn war chariots were usually manned by three soldiers, a driver, an archer, and a shield bearer.

Around 1000 B.C., the Assyrians introduced the world's first cavalry units (soldiers who fought on horseback). Cavalrymen were outfitted in chain mail armor and leather boots. They rode bareback. It would be more than a thousand years before saddles and stirrups were invented.

The heart of the army was the infantry. Foot soldiers were mainly poor farmers and other lower-class citizens. They performed a variety of jobs, including building roads and bridges for the advancing troops, carrying messages, and storming city walls. Some infantrymen carried iron spears or leather slingshots for throwing stones. Others were armed with deadly longbows.

Assyrian king Sennacherib boasted that he "besieged and conquered" Lachish, a city in the ancient kingdom of Judah, "by the assault of foot soldiers." Reliefs on the walls of the king's palace at Nineveh provide a blow-by-blow account of the battle. Infantrymen armed with slingshots and bows march toward the

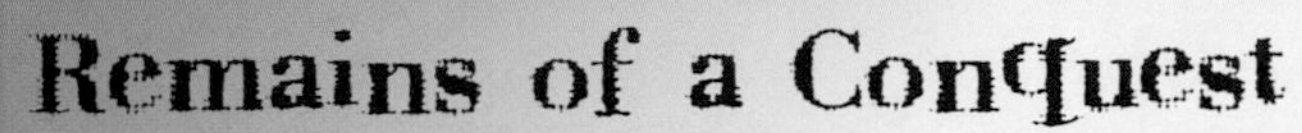

Remains of a Conquest

British archaeologists excavating the ruins of Lachish, in ancient Judah, found extensive evidence of the city's conquest by Assyrian king Sennacherib in 701 B.C. Near the main gate of the walled complex were the remains of the attackers' siege ramp, made of thousands of tons of piled stones. Scattered in the ruins of the walls were hundreds of iron arrowheads and slingshot stones. The excavators also found fragments of bronze door fittings, records of the moment when the gates were shattered by the Assyrian battering rams.

Foot soldiers were armed with a variety of weapons. The slingshots carried by these soldiers could toss stones the size of tennis balls.

walled city. They fight their way up a siege ramp under a hail of stones and arrows fired by the defenders. An inscription describes the final scene: "Sennacherib, king of all, king of Assyria, sitting on his throne while the spoils from the city of Lachish pass before him."

Marked for Slavery

Foreigners who were captured in war and spared execution were often forced into slavery. Mesopotamia also had a number of native-born slaves. These were mainly citizens who had been forced to sell themselves, and sometimes their entire families, into slavery to pay off their debts.

Most slaves were owned by the temples or palaces. They worked alongside free laborers on large-scale building and maintenance projects. Rich families also owned slaves. These household slaves usually worked as servants, performing chores such as cooking, weaving, and gardening.

The law permitted masters to beat their slaves. However, according to the Code of Hammurabi, if a slave should "strike the body of a freed man, his ear shall be cut off." The penalties were even harsher for free citizens who stole slaves or helped them run away. Hammurabi's laws decreed that anyone caught hiding a runaway slave should be put to death. If a barber cut off the *abbuttu* (the distinctive topknot of hair that marked a slave) "without the knowledge of [the slave's] master . . . the hands of this barber shall be cut off."

While foreign captives were usually enslaved for life, native-born slaves had at least a hope of gaining their freedom. Slaves who were born into a household were often freed after their owner's death. Those who knew a trade might be permitted to set up their own shops. Paying their owners a portion of their income and keeping the rest, they could eventually earn enough money to buy their freedom.

Another path to freedom was offered by the decrees of "justice" or "righteousness" sometimes issued by kings at the beginning of their reign. These charitable proclamations freed all citizens from debt slavery. The earliest example comes from the reign of Enmetena, king of the Sumerian city-state of Lagash. Around 2400 B.C., a royal inscription announced that the king had "annulled debts for Lagash, restoring mother to child and restoring child to mother."

A relief from Assurbanipal's palace at Nineveh shows the king's victorious troops leading a procession of war prisoners. Foreign captives whose lives were spared were usually enslaved for life.

DOCTORS AND SCIENTISTS

The people of Mesopotamia carefully observed the world around them, so that they could better understand and serve the gods. In the process they made remarkable discoveries that improved their lives and led to the birth of some of our modern sciences.

Nearly everything we know about Mesopotamian science comes from clay tablets discovered in palaces, temples, and libraries. These ancient texts reveal a curious blend of religion, superstition, and practical knowledge.

Medical Magic

The ancient Mesopotamians believed that illness was caused by the gods and demons as a punishment for sins. Two kinds of doctors offered sick people two very different cures.

*Ashipu*s relied on magic. They studied a patient's symptoms and then performed rituals and incantations to drive out the visiting demon. These doctors referred to medical texts outlining ways to purge the demons responsible for specific

Sometimes plaques were created to ward off the evil demons that were believed to cause illness. In this plaque a sick person is attended by "fish-men," mythical creatures with magical protecive powers.

An Ancient Prescription

Nearly four thousand years ago, a Sumerian *asu* wrote down a few of his favorite prescriptions. In the early 1900s archaeologists unearthed his tablet in the ruins of Nippur. No one knows if the doctor's medicines worked or even what diseases they were supposed to cure. However, the ancient remedies have taught historians a great deal about the "practical" branch of Mesopotamian medicine. Here is one of the doctor's prescriptions for a **poultice** (medicated dressing):

> Sift and knead together . . . turtle-shell, the sprouting naga plant and mustard; wash the sick spot with quality beer and hot water; scrub the sick spot with all of the kneaded mixture; after scrubbing, rub with vegetable oil and cover with pulverized fir.

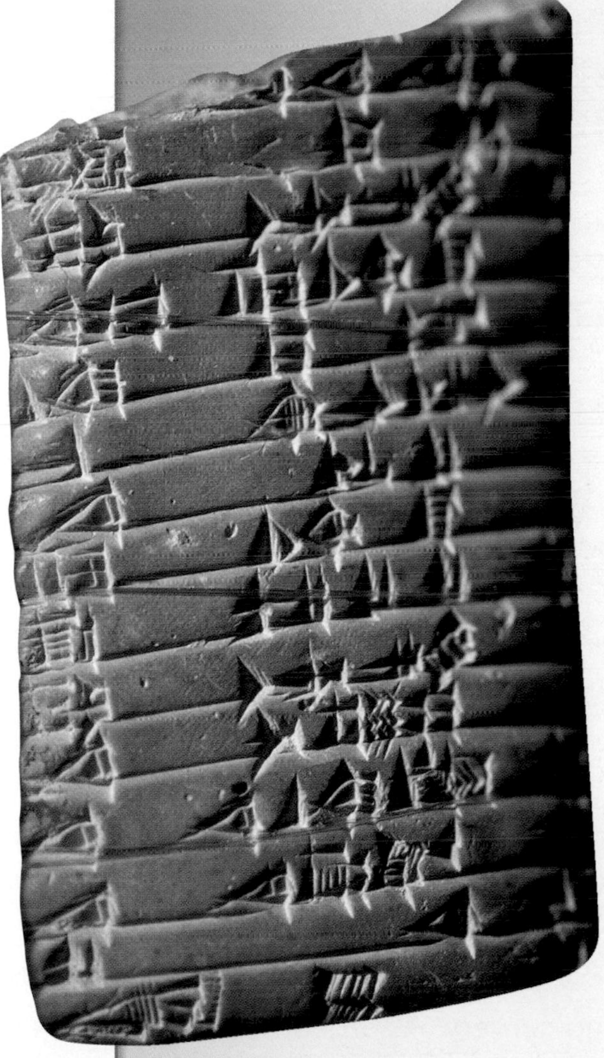

A replica of an ancient clay tablet shows a medical prescription in cuneiform, the writing system used in ancient Mesopotamia.

conditions. To treat a patient with epilepsy, one text advised, the doctor should place "the little finger of a dead man, rancid oil, and copper into the skin of a virgin goat; you shall string it on a tendon of a gerbil and put it round his neck, and he will recover."

Asus practiced a somewhat more practical form of medicine. The texts used by these healers listed medications to treat hundreds of different illnesses, including headaches, ear infections, lice, tonsillitis, and smallpox. Remedies were derived mainly from herbs and other plants. An *asu* might apply his medicines in ointments or dressings or prepare a potion for the patient to drink. Foul-tasting medicines were often dissolved in beer.

The Doctor's Practice

Most Mesopotamian doctors were men. Women often served as midwives, assisting in pregnancy and childbirth. During a difficult delivery, the midwife might massage the mother's belly with ointment or a rolling pin made of magic wood. She also chanted incantations. One plea to the god Marduk ended, "Bring forth that sealed-up one, a creature of the gods, as a human creature; let him come forth! Let him see the light!"

Some professional healers worked for the palaces or temples, while others treated ordinary citizens. The Code of Hammurabi outlined fees for different medical services, in amounts that varied according to the patient's social status. A doctor who healed "the broken bone or diseased soft part" of an upper-class citizen could charge five **shekels** (units of silver). A commoner paid three shekels for the same service. The owner of a sick slave paid just two shekels.

There were also rewards, as well as alarming penalties, for the few doctors who practiced surgery. A surgeon who "opened an eye-infection with a bronze instrument and so saved the man's eye" was entitled to ten shekels. However, if he "thereby destroyed the man's eye, they shall cut off his hand."

Math Wizards

The Sumerians began writing numbers around 3100 B.C. Over time Mesopotamian mathematicians developed a sophisticated

A Sumerian clay tablet shows the calculations used to figure out the surface area of a piece of land. This tablet was created sometime around 2100 B.C.

number system based on 60, which they used for counting, weighing, and measuring. Today their invention survives in our 360-degree circle and 60-minute hour.

Archaeologists have found hundreds of tablets filled with mathematical calculations. Some are tables, with rows and columns of numbers. These were used to work out practical problems, such as the area of a farm field, the volume of water in a canal, or the interest due on a loan. Other clay tablets contained math exercises used in schools. Mesopotamian students scratched their heads over complex word problems much like those in modern-day textbooks. Instead of computing the speed of a train, however, they had to figure out how long it would take workers to dig a canal or build a palace.

Observing the Heavens

Today we draw a sharp line between **astronomy** (the scientific study of the stars, planets, and other heavenly bodies) and **astrology,** which is based on the belief that the heavens

An astronomical tablet from the Sumerian city-state of Kish records the rising and setting of Venus over a period of six years.

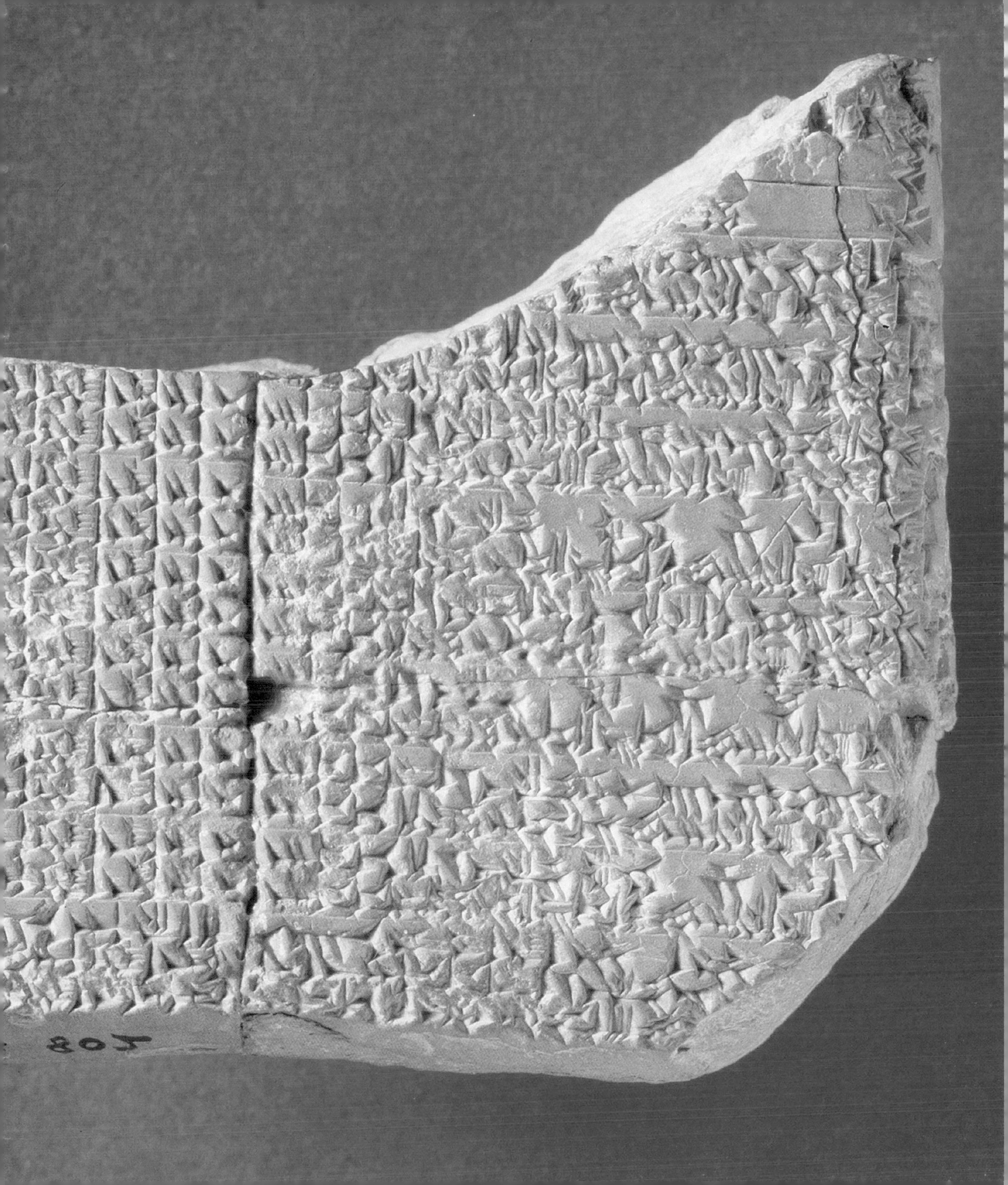

The Babylonian World Map

The Mesopotamians believed that the earth was a flat disk topped by the dome of the heavens. That view of the world is reflected in the Babylonian world map. Created around 600 B.C., this ancient clay tablet shows the round disk of the world, with Babylon at its center. Encircling the world is the Earthly Ocean. Beyond the ocean lie the Seven Islands, drawn as triangles around the edge of the circle.

Inscriptions on the tablet explain that the Seven Islands include wondrous lands where fierce beasts dwell and "the sun is not seen." The islands form bridges to the Heavenly Ocean, which holds the constellations. According to a Babylonian myth, the gods who created the world dwelled in the heavens in the form of animals.

influence human affairs. In ancient Mesopotamia the two were inseparable.

The people of Mesopotamia believed that the gods lived in the heavens. It was only logical to search the stars for clues to divine wishes and intentions. In observatories scattered throughout the kingdom, priests and other learned men watched over the heavens day and night. Using simple tools such as hollow tubes, sundials, and clocks that marked time with water or shadows, they made remarkably accurate observations.

The earliest records of the work of these stargazers are the "Venus tablets," which were written in the seventeenth century B.C. This collection of clay tablets contained astronomical observations of Venus, along with astrological interpretations of the meaning behind the planet's movements. One tablet reads, "Venus disappeared in the west. Three days it stayed away, then . . . it became visible in the east. Springs will open and Adad [the thunder god] will bring his rain and Ea [the water god] his floods."

Mesopotamian astronomers developed a twelve-month calendar based on the cycles of the moon. They compiled lists of the stars and named the constellations. Dividing the sky into twelve segments in an imaginary band called the zodiac, astrologers wrote the first horoscopes. These foretold a baby's future based on the position of the stars in the zodiac at the time of his or her birth.

Some time around the eighth century B.C., the Mesopotamians brought their sophisticated mathematics to the study of the skies. Soon they were able to calculate the distances between the stars and predict many heavenly events. Archaeologists have found astronomical almanacs plotting the future positions of the sun, moon, stars, and planets for periods as long as fifty years.

SCRIBES AND POETS

Most scholars believe that the greatest achievement in Mesopotamian history was the invention of writing. In fact, there *was* no history until writing was invented, because history is a written record of the past. Learning to write made it possible to record events, experiences, thoughts, and wisdom for future generations.

The earliest known writing appears on clay tablets from around 3300 B.C. The tablets were discovered in a temple in the Sumerian city of Uruk. Temple officials needed a way to keep track of business, such as goods produced, gifts sent by citizens, and wages issued to workers. At first they used a variety of small clay tokens. To record a gift of six sheep, a priest might place six cone-shaped tokens inside a clay ball.

Soon the record keepers found an easier system. Instead of counting out tokens, they made impressions by pressing the tokens into soft clay tablets. Other markings were added to keep track of an increasing variety of goods. The first of these markings were word-pictures known as **pictographs**. The pictograph for cattle was a simple drawing of a bull's head. For grain, it was an ear of barley.

A Sumerian clay tablet shows the early use of word-pictures to record information.

The Rock of Behistun

For years historians knew that the key to Mesopotamia's past lay in the wedge-shaped marks called cuneiform. Many tried without success to decipher the mysterious writing. Then, in the 1840s, a British army officer and scholar named Henry Rawlinson made a breakthrough. Rawlinson was fascinated by huge reliefs carved on the face of a cliff near Behistun, Iran. Alongside figures of mighty kings was a 1,306-line message. Rawlinson scaled the sheer cliff several times, perching on narrow ledges to copy the inscription. Back in his office in Baghdad, with his pet lion cub at his feet, he finally cracked the code and translated the writings. His work enabled scholars to read the language of the Babylonians and Assyrians, unlocking many of the secrets of these ancient civilizations.

Eventually the pictographs developed into hundreds of "shorthand" symbols. These combinations of wedge-shaped marks could be drawn with a few strokes of a **stylus**, a blunt instrument made from a marsh reed. Some of the symbols stood for objects, others for sounds or ideas. They became the building blocks of the first writing system, known as **cuneiform**, from the Latin word for "wedge."

School Days

Cuneiform was a complicated writing system. There were more than six hundred different symbols, all with several possible meanings. Except for a few well-educated kings and nobles, the only Mesopotamians who could read and write were professional scribes.

Scribes came from well-to-do families. A collection of documents from around 2000 B.C. lists five hundred scribes, along

Because of the complexity of cuneiform, learning to become a scribe was challenging. An inscription on the back of this small stone statue identifies the figure as Dudu, a Sumerian scribe of the twenty-fifth century B.C.

with the occupations of their fathers, who included temple administrators, governors, military officers, and other important nobles. Most scribes were men. A small number of upper-class women served as scribes for communities of priestesses.

Girls training to become scribes were probably educated at home by private tutors. Boys attended a school called the *edubba*, or "tablet house." Tens of thousands of clay tablets containing exams, essays, and other texts have given historians a look inside these scribal schools.

Boys started school between the ages of five and seven. They attended every day, from sunrise to sunset, with six days off per month. The subjects they studied included reading, writing, grammar, math, science, medicine, law, and music. Scribal students learned mainly by copying exercises written out by their teachers. These included grammar lessons, math tables, and long lists of words grouped in categories such as gods, animals, plants, stones, and stars. Archaeologists have found hundreds of round school tablets showing a teacher's writing on one side and a student's work on the other.

Discipline was strict. In a four-thousand-year-old essay called "Schooldays," one graduate recalled a particularly bad day at the *edubba.* As a struggling student, he had been caned by several different teachers for tardiness, poor penmanship, talking without permission, and other offenses. Finally he "began to hate the scribal art." So he persuaded his father to invite the school's headmaster home for a fine feast and "a bit of extra salary." The tactic was successful. At the end of the evening, the headmaster turned to the student and proclaimed, "You have carried out well the school's activities, you are a man of learning. . . . Of your friends may you be their leader, may you rank the highest among the school graduates."

Everyday Wisdom

One of the favorite exercises of Mesopotamian school students was copying proverbs. Scribes collected and organized hundreds of these popular sayings. Many still strike a familiar chord today.

Into an open mouth, a fly enters.

Friendship lasts a day, kinship forever.

The traveler from distant places is an everlasting liar.

Wealth is hard to come by, but poverty is always at hand.

Who possesses much silver may be happy; who possesses much barley may be glad; but he who has nothing at all may sleep.

You can have a lord, you can have a king, but the man to fear is the tax collector!

Letters and Libraries

The young men who completed their years of study at the *edubba* became respected professionals, often holding high offices in the temples or palaces. Scribes performed many different jobs. They kept accounts and court records. They wrote out royal inscriptions, proclamations, laws, and military dispatches. Temple scribes recorded sacrificial omens. Archaeologists have unearthed tens of thousands of clay tablets analyzing the omens found in the livers of sacrificed animals.

Private scribes often managed business affairs for merchants and other clients. The tablets discovered in the Assyrian merchant colony at Kanesh include thousands of letters opening with this standard formula: "Tell Mr. ___, Mr. ___ sends the following message" (with the correspondents' names filling in the blanks). Such

Letters were often placed inside clay envelopes and closed with seals to keep the message private. The letter at the right is from a man to his brother, complaining about the approaching winter and the hardships facing his family. On the left is the envelope. The oval at the top is another page of the letter.

letters were dictated to a professional scribe by the sender and read to the recipient by another scribe.

Letters were often placed inside clay envelopes for protection. When a tablet arrived, the recipient checked to make sure that the envelope was still closed and marked with the sender's cylinder seal. That way correspondents could be certain that no one had read or tampered with their private letters.

Merchants and nobles often stored their tablets at home inside pottery jars, reed baskets, or wooden chests. In temple and palace libraries, large collections of texts were kept on benches or shelves. The most famous collection was the library of Assyrian king Assurbanipal at Nineveh. In the seventh century B.C., the king sent out agents with instructions to "gather together and bring to me valuable tablets of which there are no copies in Assyria. . . . If you should hear of any . . . text which seems suitable for the palace library seek it out, take it with you, and send it hither."

In the 1850s, British archaeologists excavated the ruins of Assurbanipal's palace. They found a vast store of nearly 25,000 clay tablets. The texts included writings on religion, medicine, and science, organized by subject and catalogued. This treasurehouse of ancient knowledge also included copies of many of Mesopotamia's greatest works of literature.

Tales of Gods and Heroes

Written literature was born in Sumer some five thousand years ago. Mesopotamian literature fell into several different categories, including hymns, myths, and epics. Scribes composed these literary works in the form of poetry. Their writings were chanted or recited to the accompaniment of musical instruments, such as harps, **lyres,** pipes, and drums.

Among the earliest works of literature were hymns to the gods. Some of the finest hymns were composed by the Sumerian priestess Enheduanna, a daughter of King Sargon. More than four thousand years ago, the priestess composed a set of hymns to the goddess Inanna. In her writings she identified herself by name, becoming the world's first known author:

> En-hedu-anna am I, I will now say a prayer to you.
> My tears, like sweet beer
> I now shed them freely for you, fate-determining Inanna.

Mesopotamian myths told tales of the gods. One of the best-known myths was the *Enuma Elish*. In this Babylonian creation story, Marduk formed the sky, the earth, and a race of men, who were "charged with the service of the gods that they might be at ease."

Another famous myth was the *Atrahasis*, sometimes called the Mesopotamian Flood Story. In this ancient Babylonian tale, written around 1700 B.C., the gods punished humankind by sending a terrible storm "so that the water rose above the mountains." One righteous mortal, a king named Utnapishtim, built a boat and saved his family, along with "the seed of all living creatures." Many historians believe that the biblical story of Noah and the ark was inspired by the *Atrahasis*.

Mesopotamian poets also wrote epics. The most famous of these long narrative poems about legendary heroes was the *Epic of Gilgamesh*. A seventh-century B.C. version of this collection of tales was discovered in Assurbanipal's library at Nineveh, inscribed on twelve large clay tablets.

The *Epic of Gilgamesh* describes the adventures of a superhuman king who sets out to find the secret of eternal life. During his quest, Gilgamesh faces incredible perils and performs many daring deeds. At last he accepts the fact that victory over death is impossible and returns home, a wiser and kinder ruler.

The Epic of Gilgamesh

The *Epic of Gilgamesh* has been called the world's first great work of literature. In this passage, translated by historian Samuel Kramer, an innkeeper tries to persuade the hero to abandon his search for immortality.

> Gilgamesh, whither are you wandering?
> Life, which you look for, you will never find.
> For when the gods created man, they let
> Death be his share, and withheld life
> In their own hands.
> Gilgamesh, fill your belly—
> Day and night make merry,
> Let days be full of joy.
> Dance and make music day and night,
> And wear fresh clothes.
> And wash your head and bathe.
> Look at the child that is holding your hand,
> And let your wife delight in your embrace.
> These things alone are the concern of men.

A tablet from the seventh century B.C. shows part of the *Epic of Gilgamesh*.

THE LEGACY OF ANCIENT MESOPOTAMIA

In 539 B.C. the armies of Cyrus the Great, ruler of the Persian Empire, marched into Babylon. The Babylonian king, Nabonidus, was weak and unpopular. When he surrendered without a fight, the people of Babylon welcomed Cyrus as a liberator. That marked the end of some three thousand years of political independence for Mesopotamia.

Although the ancient civilizations of this region came to an end, their ideas and inventions lived on. During Mesopotamia's many centuries of power, its culture influenced both neighboring countries and distant trading partners. Historians have traced its impact in the art, architecture, political organization, religion, and literature of ancient Egypt, Persia, India, and many other parts of the Eastern world.

Mesopotamian culture also found its way to the West. The ancient Hebrews, carried into exile by Nebuchadrezzar in the sixth century B.C., absorbed many aspects of Babylonian learning and literature. They preserved these influences in their traditions and holy writings, many of which carried over into

Christianity and the Western world. Ancient Greece was another important link in the chain connecting Mesopotamia with the West. The Greeks conquered Persia in the third century B.C. Many of the great achievements of ancient Greek writers, artists, architects, philosophers, and scientists were inspired by the remnants of Mesopotamian civilization. Later, the Romans and other conquerors carried this legacy across the world, down the centuries, to touch our lives today.

What did the people of ancient Sumer, Babylonia, and Assyria contribute to our modern world? The list is almost endless. It includes practical inventions such as the wheel, the plow, and the

Many important elements of our daily life can be traced back to Mesopotamia. Just try to imagine what our world would be like without the wheel!

Many artifacts from ancient Mesopotamia have been damaged or lost during military conflicts in Iraq. U.S. soldiers are shown here patrolling the National Museum of Iraq.

use of the arch in architecture. The Mesopotamians gave us writing, cities, the concept of kingship, government bureaucracy, and organized religion. They shaped our ideas of law and justice through the Code of Hammurabi and earlier collections of written law. They developed mathematics, medicine, and astronomy. Whenever we search the night skies for a constellation, we are looking at patterns of stars named by the Babylonians. When we look at a clock, read a horoscope, or ride a bicycle, we reach back in time to the ancient land between the rivers.

Today the only hard evidence of Mesopotamia's primary role in world history comes from the artifacts and ruins discovered by archaeologists. Scholars from around the world, including many in Iraq, have worked hard to uncover and preserve these valuable clues to the past.

Unfortunately, many archaeological treasures have been lost in recent warfare. During the Iran-Iraq War of 1980–1988 and the Persian Gulf War of 1991, a number of archaeological sites were damaged, and many artifacts were stolen from museums. In 2003 the Iraq War brought further devastation. The worst losses took place at the National Museum in Baghdad. There some ten thousand ancient artifacts, including priceless objects dating back more than seven thousand years, were smashed or stolen by looters. While scholars have recovered some of the stolen artifacts, most were lost forever.

Four thousand years ago, a Mesopotamian poet mourned the fall of Sumerian civilization in "Lamentation over the Destruction of Sumer and Ur." His words are a fitting lament for the modern-day losses in the cradle of civilization.

My silver, gems and lapis-lazuli
have verily been scattered about—let me cry "Oh my possessions!"
My silver—men who had never known silver
have verily filled their hands with it.
My gems—men who had never known gems
have verily hung them around their necks.

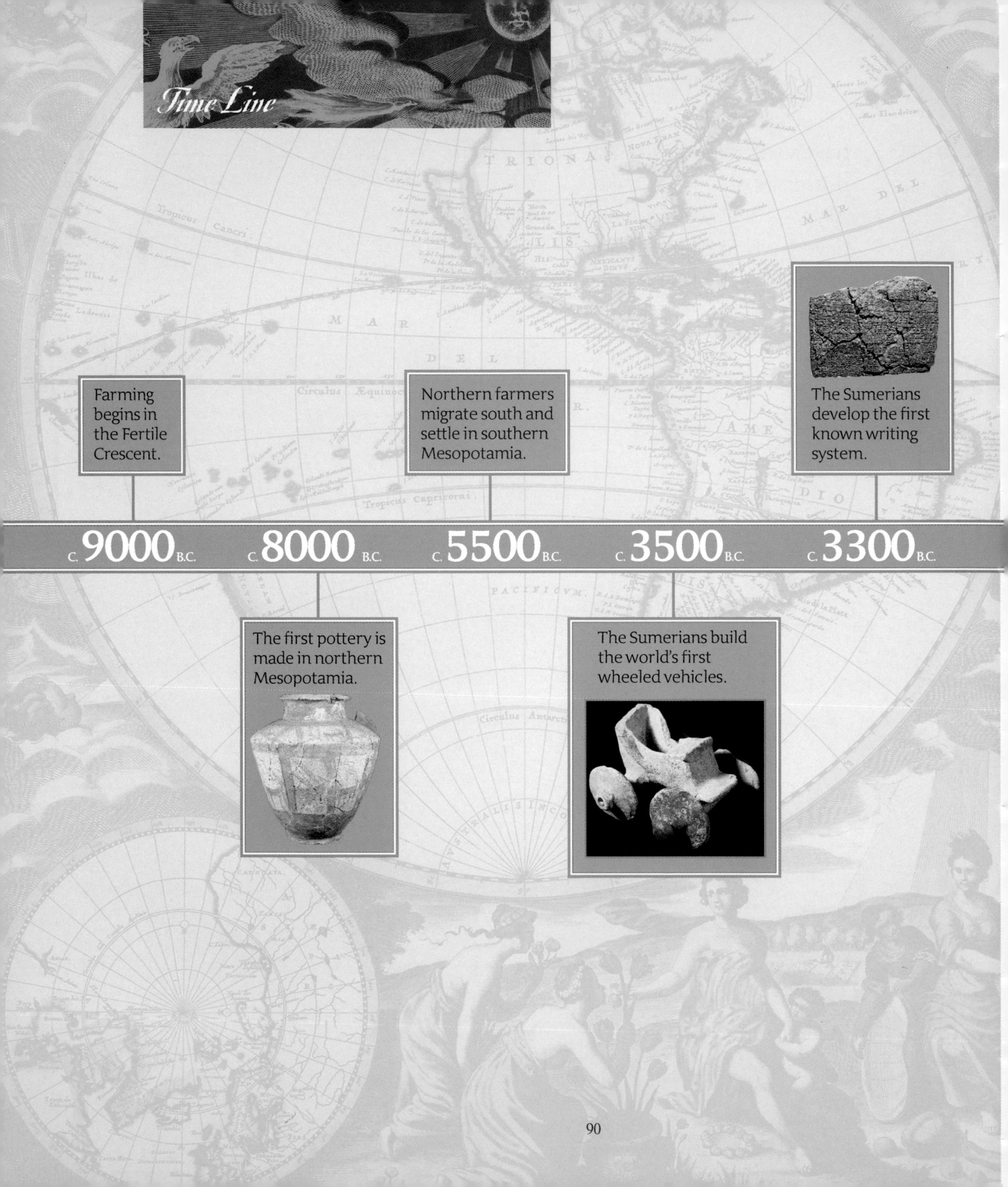

Time Line

c. 9000 B.C.
Farming begins in the Fertile Crescent.

c. 8000 B.C.
The first pottery is made in northern Mesopotamia.

c. 5500 B.C.
Northern farmers migrate south and settle in southern Mesopotamia.

c. 3500 B.C.
The Sumerians build the world's first wheeled vehicles.

c. 3300 B.C.
The Sumerians develop the first known writing system.

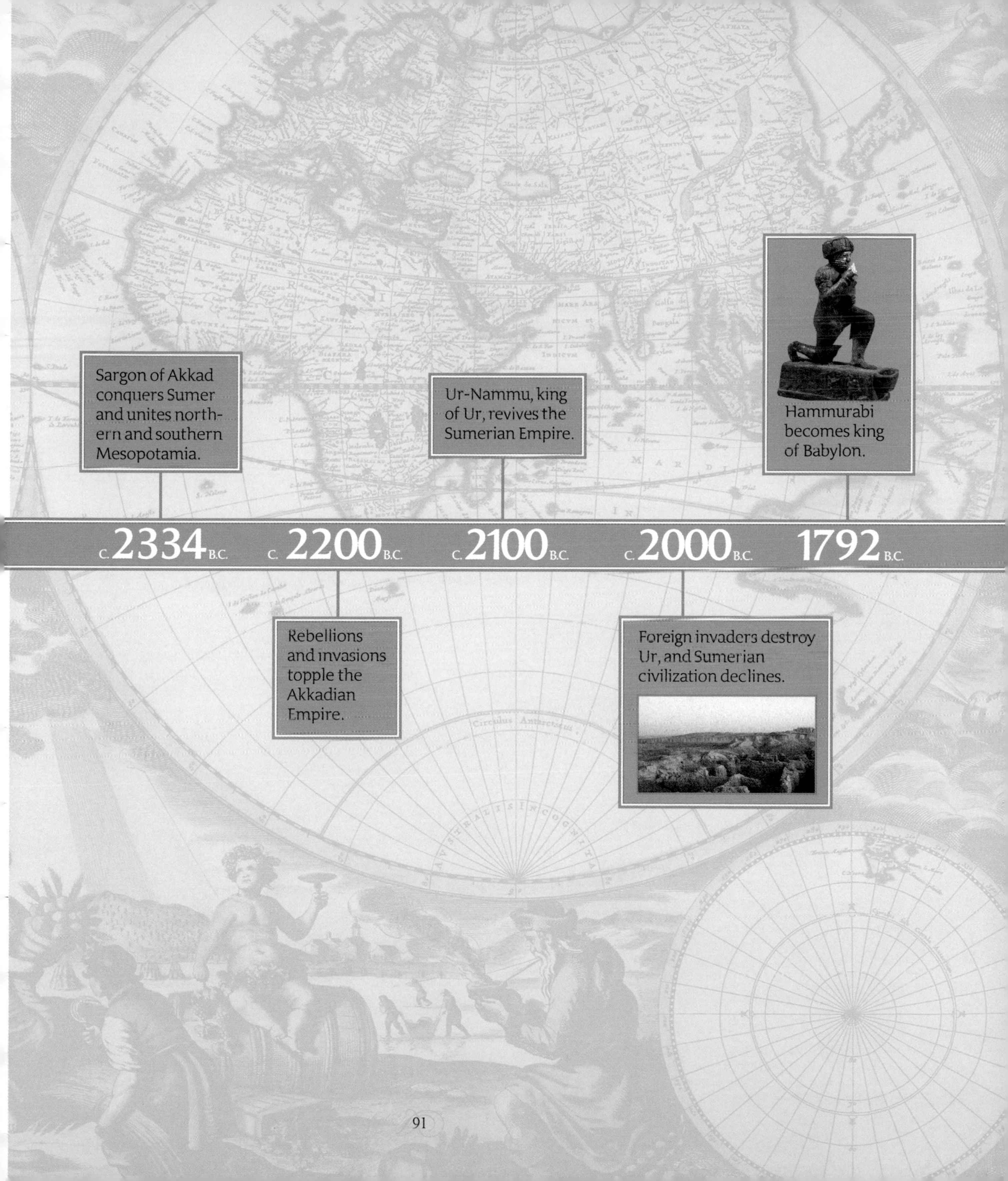

Sargon of Akkad conquers Sumer and unites northern and southern Mesopotamia.

c. 2334 B.C.

Rebellions and invasions topple the Akkadian Empire.

c. 2200 B.C.

Ur-Nammu, king of Ur, revives the Sumerian Empire.

c. 2100 B.C.

Foreign invaders destroy Ur, and Sumerian civilization declines.

c. 2000 B.C.

Hammurabi becomes king of Babylon.

1792 B.C.

c. 1760 B.C. — The Code of Hammurabi is engraved in stone.

c. 1700 B.C. — The *Atrahasis*, sometimes known as the Mesopotamian Flood Story, is written.

c. 1595 B.C. — Babylon is sacked by foreign invaders.

c. 1365 B.C. — The Assyrian Empire rises to power.

c. 1000 B.C. — The Assyrians introduce the world's first cavalry units.

c. 701 B.C. — Assyrian king Sennacherib conquers the city-state of Lachish in Judah.

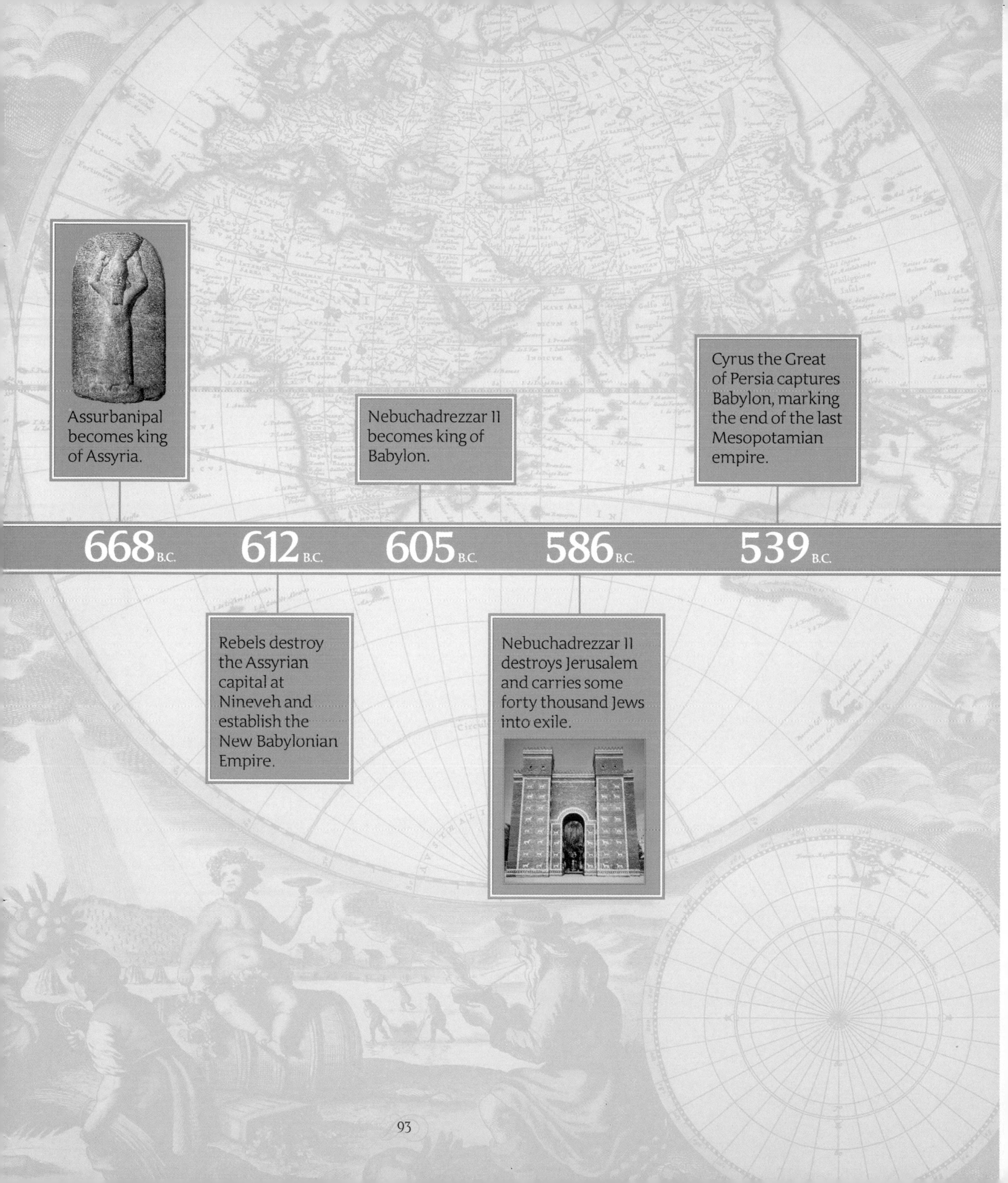

Assurbanipal becomes king of Assyria.

668 B.C.

612 B.C.

Rebels destroy the Assyrian capital at Nineveh and establish the New Babylonian Empire.

605 B.C.

Nebuchadrezzar II becomes king of Babylon.

586 B.C.

Nebuchadrezzar II destroys Jerusalem and carries some forty thousand Jews into exile.

539 B.C.

Cyrus the Great of Persia captures Babylon, marking the end of the last Mesopotamian empire.

Assurbanipal (ah-soor-BAH-nuh-pahl)

ruled 668-627 B.C.

The last great king of the Assyrian Empire, Assurbanipal was known for his fierceness in battle. He built magnificent temples and palaces in his capital at Nineveh. He also assembled one of the first systematically collected and organized libraries, containing works of literature and texts on science, medicine, religion, and magic.

Assurnasirpal II (ah-soor-NAH-zir-pahl)

ruled 883-859 B.C.

Assurnasirpal II was one of the first warrior-kings of Assyria. He extended the Assyrian Empire as far north as Urartu (in eastern Turkey) and as far west as the Mediterranean Sea. He built a magnificent palace at Calah (present-day Nimrud, Iraq).

Enheduanna (en-hed-yoo-ON-uh)

c. 2250-2300 B.C.

Enheduanna was high priestess at the Sumerian city-state of Ur and a daughter of King Sargon of Assad. She was the world's first author known by name. Her writings included forty-two brief hymns about temples and three long, intricate hymns to the goddess Inanna.

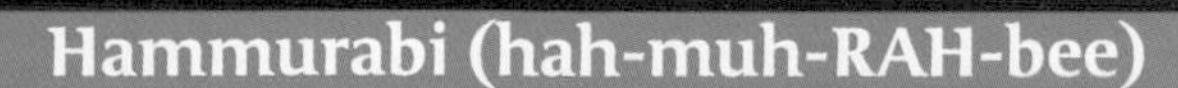

Hammurabi (hah-muh-RAH-bee)

ruled 1792-1750 B.C.

The founder of the Babylonian Empire, Hammurabi ruled his large kingdom from his capital at Babylon. He built a number of temples and other structures and promoted advances in agriculture, irrigation, and navigation. The Code of Hammurabi, a collection of some three hundred laws, is one of the ancient world's most famous legal codes.

Ku-Bau

ruled c. 2400 B.C.

Ku-Bau was the only known female ruler of a Sumerian city-state. According to the Sumerian King List, she ruled Kish for one hundred years. Her name is also spelled Kug-Bau or Ku-Baba.

Nabonidus (nab-un-I-dus)

ruled 556-539 B.C.

Nabonidus was king of the Babylonian Empire and the last king of Mesopotamia. He was an unpopular monarch who left Babylon and lived in Arabia for ten years, appointing his son to rule in his place. When the empire was invaded by Cyrus the Great in 539, Nabonidus returned to Babylon but was captured. His fate is unknown.

Nebuchadrezzar II (neh-byuh-kuh-DREH-zer)

ruled 605-562 B.C.

Nebuchadrezzar restored Mesopotamian control over Palestine and Syria and captured Jerusalem, carrying thousands of Jews into exile. His conquests brought great prosperity to the kingdom, and he built many splendid palaces, temples, and shrines in Babylon. He was the last great king of the New Babylonian Empire.

Puabi

c. 2600-2500 B.C.

Puabi was a Sumerian queen who was buried at Ur. Her tomb contained many treasures, including jewelry and art objects made of gold, silver, ivory, and precious stones. She was buried with hundreds of attendants, who had poisoned themselves to continue to serve her in the afterworld.

Sargon of Akkad

ruled c. 2334

Sargon was the first king to unite all of Mesopotamia under a single ruler. He conquered all of northern and southern Mesopotamia and parts of Syria, Anatolia, and Elam (western Iran). His capital at Agade has never been found.

Sennacherib (suh-NAH-kuh-rub)

ruled 705-681 B.C.

This powerful Assyrian king captured Babylon and dozens of cities in ancient Palestine. His failed attempt to capture Jerusalem is recorded in the Bible. Sennacherib built Nineveh into one of the ancient world's most splendid capitals.

Shamshi-Adad I

ruled c. 1813–1780 B.C.

Shamshi-Adad was a powerful Assyrian king who united northern Mesopotamia. He ruled a domain stretching from western Iran to the Mediterranean Sea. In the later years of his rule, he appointed his two sons to serve as lesser kings.

Glossary

Anatolia the part of modern-day Turkey that includes the Asia Minor peninsula

antiquities pottery, writing tablets, statues, and other artifacts from ancient times

archaeologists scientists who study the physical remains of past cultures to learn about human life and activity

artifacts objects from a particular period of history

astrology the practice of predicting the supposed influence of the stars and planets on human affairs

astronomy the scientific study of the sun, moon, stars, and other heavenly bodies

bureaucracy a complex government system with many levels of departments and officials

caravans groups of people and pack animals traveling together, often across a desert or through dangerous lands

cereals plants such as wheat or barley, which have grains that are used for food

concubines the "secondary wives" of a king or high-ranking noble, who had a lower status and fewer rights than the principal wife

crown prince the man who is next in line to the throne

cuneiform (KYOO-nuh-form) a system of writing made up of characters formed from wedge-shaped strokes; from the Latin word *cuneus*, or "wedge"

domesticated trained or adapted an animal so that it would live close to people and be useful to them

dynasties ruling families that pass down their authority from generation to generation

Fertile Crescent an arc-shaped section of land in the Middle East that included parts of modern-day Israel, Jordan, Lebanon, Syria, Turkey, Iraq, and Iran. In ancient times the Fertile Crescent was a rich food-growing region.

infantrymen the foot soldiers of an army

inscriptions words written or engraved on stone, metal, or another hard surface

irrigate to supply water to crops using channels, pumps, or other artificial means

lapis lazuli a sparkling blue semiprecious stone

lyres stringed musical instruments similar to harps, with a U-shaped frame

mina an ancient unit of weight equal to about 18 ounces (504 grams)

mosaic a picture or design made from small pieces of colored tile, stone, glass, or other materials

omens occurrences that are believed to be signs of future events

patron god a deity that was believed to be a city's special protector

pictographs pictures used to represent words or ideas

poultice a medicated dressing used to treat aches, sores, inflammation, and other conditions

reliefs sculptures in which the figures stand out from a flat background

shekels small pieces of silver with a specific weight (about one-third of an ounce, or 8 grams), used in Mesopotamia as money

siege the surrounding of a fort or city, during which the attackers cut off food and other supplies to force the enemy to surrender

stylus an instrument with a wedge-shaped tip that was used for writing on clay or waxed tablets

tells ancient mounds of earth in the Middle East containing the ruins of settlements

tribute a payment given by one ruler or country to another as a sign of respect and submission

ziggurats tall pyramid-shaped structures with a shrine or temple at the top

To Find Out More

Books

Greene, Jacqueline Dembar. *Slavery in Ancient Egypt and Mesopotamia.* Danbury, CT: Franklin Watts, 2000.

Haywood, John. *World Atlas of the Past.* Volume 1, *The Ancient World.* New York: Oxford University Press, 2000.

Hunter, Erica C. D. *First Civilizations.* New York: Facts on File, 1994.

Malam, John. *Mesopotamia and the Fertile Crescent, 10,000 to 539 B.C.* Austin, TX: Raintree Steck-Vaughn, 1999.

Moss, Carol. *Science in Ancient Mesopotamia.* New York: Franklin Watts, 1998.

Nardo, Don. *Empires of Mesopotamia.* San Diego, CA: Lucent Books, 2001.

Service, Pamela F. *Mesopotamia.* New York: Marshall Cavendish, 1999.

Organizations and Online Sites

Ancient Art: Mesopotamia
http://www.dia.org/collections/ancient/mesopotamia/mesopotamia.html

This online exhibit includes selected items from the collection of ancient Mesopotamian pottery and sculpture at the Detroit Institute of Arts.

Ancient Civilizations: Mesopotamia
http://www.mesopotamia.co.uk/menu.html

Developed by the British Museum, this excellent site contains lots of interesting information on writing, geography, religion, warfare, and other aspects of Mesopotamian society. Click on the "Explore" link for interactive games.

Ancient Mesopotamia
http://www.providence.edu/dwc/mesopot.htm

Created by Providence College in Providence, Rhode Island, this Web site offers links to sites with information on topics including art and archaeology, history, mathematics, mythology, and religion.

Ancient Tablets, Ancient Graves: Accessing Women's Lives in Mesopotamia
http://www.womeninworldhistory.com/lesson2.html

Learn about women's lives in ancient Mesopotamia. The site offers quotes from clay tablets and other artifacts, as well as study questions and answers.

Archaeological Sites: Ur
http://www.mnsu.edu/emuseum/archaeology/sites/middle_east/ur.html

Created by the University of Pennsylvania Museum of Archaeology and Anthropology, this site features information on discoveries in the Sumerian city-state of Ur.

The Code of Hammurabi
http://www.yale.edu/lawweb/avalon/medieval/hammenu.htm

Read the laws established by Hammurabi, as translated by historian L. W. King.

The Electronic Text Corpus of Sumerian Literature
http://www-etcsl.orient.ox.ac.uk/

Created by the Oriental Institute at the University of Oxford in Oxford, England, this site provides translations of hundreds of ancient Sumerian texts. Click on the "Browse by category" link to find letters, hymns, prayers, and other types of literature.

Internet Ancient History Sourcebook: Mesopotamia
http://www.fordham.edu/halsall/ancient/asbook03.html

This online resource provides links to Web sites with a wide variety of information on different periods in Mesopotamian history. This is a good source for locating maps and translations of ancient myths, poems, and other texts. The site was edited by Paul Halsall.

Index

About the Author

Virginia Schomp has written more than fifty titles for young readers on topics including dinosaurs, careers, biographies, and American history. Her writings on cultures of the past include *The Ancient Greeks, Japan in the Days of the Samurai,* and *The Italian Renaissance,* as well as *The Ancient Chinese,* another title in the People of the Ancient World series. She is most intrigued by the "story" in history—the writings and remembrances that bring alive the struggles, sorrows, hopes, and dreams of people who lived long ago. Writing about ancient Mesopotamia gave her a chance to rediscover all the remarkable advances made in the "cradle of civilization," including the invention of writing itself.

Ms. Schomp earned a Bachelor of Arts degree in English Literature from the Pennsylvania State University. She lives in the Catskill Mountain region of New York.